GHARBZADEGI
[WESTSTRUCKNESS]

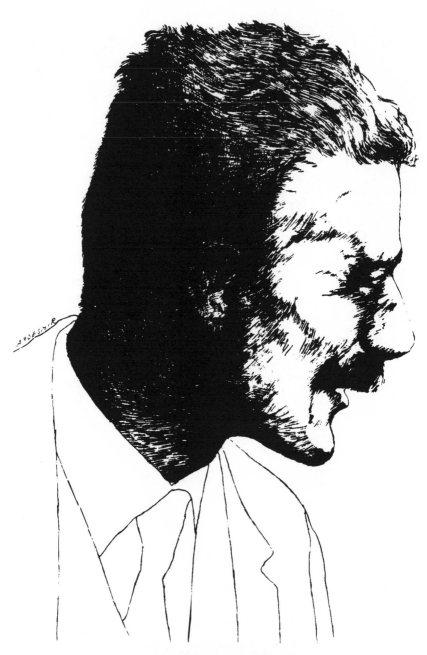

Jalal Al-e Ahmad
(1923-69)

GHARBZADEGI
[WESTSTRUCKNESS]

Jalal Al-e Ahmad

**Translated from the Persian by
John Green and Ahmad Alizadeh**

MAZDA PUBLISHERS
Costa Mesa, California
1997

Mazda Publishers
Academic publishers since 1980
A. K. Jabbari, Publisher
For information about this book contact:
www.mazdapublishers.com

Library of Congress Catalog Card No.: 82-61280
ISBN 10: 0-939214-07-5
ISBN 13: 978-0-939214-07-5
Soft cover: alk paper

8th printing, 2021   Mazda Publishers

CONTENTS:

ACKNOWLEDGMENTS

During our sporadic collaboration on this translation over the course of the past three years, we have often benefited from the advice and encouragement of friends and teachers. Thanks are due especially to Zohre Bullock, John Lorentz, and Kazem Tehrani for running an excellent Persian program at Portland State University and for helping us with all kinds of problems, including our translation. We would also like to thank Michael Hillmann of The University of Texas at Austin, who read our preliminary edition and provided much-appreciated encouragement and advice, and Ahmad Jabbari of Mazda Publishers, who has been a most meticulous and valued critic during the final preparation and revision of the manuscript. Sharon Empy of Portland State University has reviewed the entire translation and helped us spot a good many errors and omissions, for which we are very grateful. Assistance in obtaining text-processing resources has been supplied by the Center for Near Eastern and North African Studies at the University of Michigan. We would particularly like to thank K. Allin Luther, Mary Ringia, and Kathleen Wilson for being there at the right times with what we needed. The inevitable remaining errors and shortcomings herein are, of course, solely the responsibility of the translators.

TRANSLATORS' INTRODUCTION

Jalal Al-e Ahmad (1923-69) was a shrewd and in-
sightful Iranian intellectual with numerous interests. His published legacy spans a prolific twenty-
four-year career as literary artist, translator, eth-
nologist, essayist, social and literary critic,
ideologist, teacher, and political activist.[1] The
present essay was his most popular work. It appeared
in 1962, when Al-e Ahmad was the most audible and
convincing voice of social conscience among his con-
temporaries. Gharbzadegi [Weststruckness] attained
such prominence despite the fact that secret police
(SAVAK) censorship kept it from being openly
published and distributed until 1978, and that it had
been written in an indirect and obscure style in an-
ticipation of that censorship.

In Gharbzadegi, Al-e Ahmad urged the Shi'i clergy to reassume its traditional role as the spearhead
of popular resistance to the injustices of the
secular government. A year after it appeared Ayatollah Khomeini took the first of his many dramatic
stands against the Pahlavi regime's policies, and established himself as a major voice of opposition to
the government. Al-e Ahmad anticipated the
religiously inspired uprisings of 1963 in
Gharbzadegi. His analysis accurately represented the
thinking of many Iranians. Gharbzadegi is thus a

document of immense significance for students of
Iranian social and intellectual history.

Western influence in Iran was already widely
resented when Gharbzadegi appeared. While the
government was able to sustain its operations, to
spend lavishly on weapons, and to forego taxes and
tariffs because of petroleum revenues, it did not
chose the path of economic independence. Rather,
government policy favored foreign investment and
domestic big business. The resulting conspicuous
presence and privileged status of the outsider and
the native elite inevitably gave rise to resentment
and anger. Even though Iran's overall standard of
living was higher than it had ever been, the increased social mobility that this produced only mag-
nified the inequalities and poor planning that
plagued Iranian life. Credit policies favored rich
Iranians and foreigners in both industry and agriculture, while licensing was restricted and had to be
purchased with influence at high prices by whoever
wished to export, import, or do business with the
government.[2] These policies resulted in a wide gap
between the concentrated wealth at the top of the income scale and the incomes of the majority of the
population which was either unemployed or living on
subsistence wages. The employment situation, as Al-e
Ahmad observes, could have been improved through the
encouragement of smaller enterprises and regionally
produced products, but these kinds of businesses were
denied licensing and credit by government policies,
and were undermined in any case by the creation of
'Weststruck' consumer demands that could only be
satisfied by expensive imports.

Gharbzadegi is a protest against the disastrous
consequences of Western domination for one particular
developing country as well as a portrayal of the
dynamics of native collaboration in that domination.
It is important not only for Iran but for much of the
rest of the developing world. Some of the notions
advanced in Gharbzadegi are among the assumptions
fundamental to contemporary thought in those
countries, as much to be reckoned with today as they
were twenty years ago.

Al-e Ahmad was one of the first to articulate,
for example, a widespread dislike for the Western
orientalist, who was and is seen by many as an agent
for a ruthlessly exploitative economic system. In
this view, the orientalist dehumanizes those he

'studies' by reducing them to the level of laboratory
animals. The appearance of this theme in print at a
time when the Iranian government was both encouraging
and attempting to use orientalists on an unprecedent-
ed scale was well received by a population that felt
humiliated and abused by the West. The effect was
heightened by Al-e Ahmad's argument that some of the
West's own popular heroes of the time, the
astronauts, were themselves no more than laboratory
animals for science.

        Another concept treated by Al-e Ahmad, one that
is still a basic truth in the minds of many Muslims,
is that Christian missionaries are the agents of
colonialism and neocolonial industrialization. This
idea, which is found in other third world critiques
of the West, is one of several that point to a striking similarity of outlook between Al-e Ahmad and Ivan
D. Illich. Their temperaments and backgrounds are
also comparable. Both men are antiestablishment social critics who have tried to make meaningful comparisons between Western industrial society and the
non-industrial developing societies, each writing
from the opposite vantage point, although Illich,
with the more intimate view of Western society, has
carried his analysis of industrial civilization further.[3]   Illich, like Al-e Ahmad, is a devout and
pious man--a non-practicing Catholic priest--who is
nonetheless severely critical of many of the policies
and practices of his own church. Both Illich and Al-
e Ahmad maintain that machines are the harbingers of
cognitive imperialism, that they invariably disrupt
indigenous communities, and that this is bad because
indigenous communities are the best environments for
low-cost maintenance of the dignity and sanity of
people who have been left behind in the rush to
mechanize. Each maintains that unless a society
achieves economic independence it will inevitably be
enslaved by machinery. Tools must be modifiable and
controllable by those who use them, they both say.
Each writes of the need to demythologize science.
Both men can be characterized as preindustrial con-
servatives who have the look of radicals (i.e., in
the etymological sense, as people who look for the
roots and causes of problems) and social reformers.

        Like Al-e Ahmad, Illich has a special interest
in education, a field in which both have worked
throughout their professional lives. Each has issued
a blanket condemnation of Western and Western-style
educational institutions (Illich has called teaching

"the second oldest profession"), and both have been
criticized for advocating the wholesale disassembly
of existing structures without offering much of a
replacement program. Both write from the perspective
of history with a fondness for quoting medieval sources and examples to support assertions about present
conditions. Both perceive Western society as its own
victim, and believe it to be on a collision course
with disaster. Finally, both men are temperamentally
detached and aloof, unassociated with any ideologi-
cal, political, or religious movements, but nonetheless constantly engaged in lively intellectual exchange with their peers.

Al-e Ahmad was raised in the Muslim religion as
the son of a Shi'i clergyman in Tehran, with an older
brother, two brothers-in-law, and a nephew who were
also clergymen. He was also an active and prominent
member of the leftist Tudeh party from 1944 to 1948.
He left the party shortly after it split apart due to
internal rivalries. Both as a Muslim and as a leftist he demonstrated a dislike for functioning in a
collective, organized setting. It is this aspect of
his character that has made him appear to some as
less than wholeheartedly devout and committed to his
Muslim faith.[4] It is true that he was critical of
the clergy and of Islam as practiced by the Iranian
public. He also tended to proselytize Islam on the
basis of its utilitarian features rather than on the
basis of the truth of its dogma and scripture. Yet
there is strong evidence in his own account of the
profound emotional experiences he had during his
pilgrimage to Mecca, his belief that Islam is the
only force capable of unifying Iran, the Islamic
character of the identity he develops historically
for himself, Iran, and the East, and finally his
wife's testimony to the importance of faith in his
life, that Al-e Ahmad was a sincere Muslim with no
inclination whatever to neglect or belittle the faith
itself as he understood it.

As a Muslim social critic with a knowledge of
French and English, Al-e Ahmad belonged to an intellectual class that had appeared in Iran in the latter
half of the nineteenth century. Such people have
tended to function as the culture's window on the
West, imparting to Iranian life an awareness, posi-
tively or negatively framed, of Western industrialized civilization. Many of them, including Al-e Ahmad, have displayed a certain disdain for both the
religious and secular institutions in Iran, though

not necessarily for the ideas behind them. As domestic critics, they have made tactical use of a reper-
tory of stock arguments running now against the clergy and now the state, seemingly in the interest of
maintaining a balance of power between the two. Some
of the early leaders--men like the constitutionalist
newspaper pioneer Malkum Khan--are disparaged in
Gharbzadegi for being the founders of a tradition of
which Al-e Ahmad was himself a part, as one of the
couriers of Western thought. Malkum Khan, like Al-e
Ahmad, alternately attacked and encouraged the Muslim
clergy for the sake of reformist ideals which had
been conveyed at least partly by Western sources.
Seen in this light, Al-e Ahmad can be regarded as
being very like his pro-Western predecessors in some
ways, despite the hotly anti-Western tone of
Gharbzadegi.

Although Al-e Ahmad wrote as a Muslim Iranian social critic, the numerous interests he shared with
Ivan Illich suggest that much of Gharbzadegi's essential message has been delivered in another cultural
setting by Illich. In the language of his own time
and place, Al-e Ahmad expressed an Iranian's nostal-
gia for the simplicity of bygone times in
Gharbzadegi. Like Illich, he sought to retain a
sense of self by attempting to live his life in accordance with familiar traditional values, supported
by smaller economic units, and defined by familiar
conflicts, and held the conviction that alien technology and its mass marketing are a grave threat to
the possibility of doing that. His attacks against
the West and its Iranian promoters were a response to
the West's role as the machine broker of the age,
and, as a direct consequence of that, a force
threatening to overpower and destroy Irano-Islamic
'vernacular' culture.

While Al-e Ahmad was indisputably popular, it is
difficult to say how much he influenced the actual
behavior of his compatriots. Anyone familiar with
his thinking who follows the Persian press' today,
however, is aware that in revolutionary Iran the official line on economic development is quite com-
patible with the approach he was advocating. While
spokesmen for the present government do not quote Al-
e Ahmad directly, they do make ample use of his kinds
of arguments. Village development is now a priority
objective. A Reconstruction Crusade, in some ways
the descendant of the Literacy, Health, and Development Corps of the Shah's day, is now reportedly ac-

tive in the labor-intensive construction of roads,
power lines, factories, dams, and water distribution
systems through the mobilization of unskilled rural
and urban laborers. Al-e Ahmad stressed the need for
self-sufficiency and diversification, and these are
now primary goals which have made a virtue of backwardness and a do-it-yourself-anyway approach to
problems calling for technical skill. This approach
has obviously been dictated as much by the current
war and Iran's continuing international isolation as
by inclination, however. The war with Iraq has
forced Iran to cope with the problems of repairing
and maintaining the Soviet, American, British, and
French war machines it has inherited from the Shah
and captured from the Iraqis, without the help of the
technicians and consultants who so incensed Al-e Ahmad. Economic dealings with foreign firms and
governments are generally cultivated only in cases
where parity or Iranian dominance is possible. They
sometimes involve bartering for goods and services,
and usually produce arrangements for the transfer of
technology and training into Iran.[6] In other areas,
especially education and political development, one
finds as much evidence of repression as of construc-
tive activity, although the emphasis that has been
placed on educating students in India is again one of
the things Al-e Ahmad had proposed.

Though Al-e Ahmad seemed to speak for many
Iranians, his work is quite controversial and has
been sharply criticized. He may fairly be classed as
a popular, influential, and perceptive intellectual,
but not as a scholar. By his own admission, he
"wasn't cut out" for the meticulous data collection
and systematization required of a first-rate eth-
nologist, although people do continue to find his in-
formal studies of village communities interesting.[7]
His historical assessments, again by his own admission, were hasty. They were simplistic and erroneous
at times. The Iranian historian Faridun Adamiyat has
justifiably castigated Al-e Ahmad for suggesting that
British petroleum interests were the real motivating
factor behind the Iranian Constitutional Revolution,
and for generalizing vaguely about something as
diverse and inconsistent as 'Eastern politics', to
which, according to Gharbzadegi, the West was supposedly being driven. Adamiyat even goes a step further to state that an undertaking such as Gharbzadegi
was beyond Al-e Ahmad's capabilities. For Adamiyat,
Al-e Ahmad was a mediocre writer with an inadequate
educational background, and Gharbzadegi "a sack of

straw with a few grains of wheat in it" and "nothing
more than an exercise in ignorance and stagnant dark-
ness".[1]

Adamiyat's attack is part of an intra-Iranian
controversy which has no effect on the book's value
as one representing Iranian thinking--right or wrong.
We must also add that to us as translators, there
certainly appears to be something more than ignorance
to be found in this essay, despite its manifest
deficiencies. Al-e Ahmad was a courageous activist
who saw a need to reassess history and restructure
the present in a time of social confusion. If he was
ill-equipped for the task, he had no competition at
that time from anyone with better credentials.
Moreover, his concern was urgent. Surely there must
be times when one is compelled to speak out knowing
that others--should they be so inclined--could say
what needs to be said in a better way. His ideas
were sometimes bizarre, but always worth discussing.
If we didn't always believe him, we always liked him.

THE TRANSLATION

The ideal translation needs to satisfy at least
two requirements: it should be palatable to speakers
of the target language and it should be true to the
original. 'Weststruckness', the term we have chosen
to represent __Gharbzadegi,__ was first introduced in
1974 by Michael Hillmann. It leaves something to be
desired on both the above counts, but every other
translation of this term, of which there are many,
has problems of its own. Their very abundance is
testimony to the difficulty of rendering this word
satisfactorily in English. A list of the published
versions would include Plagued by the West, Blighted
by the West, Westernization, Westmania, Westoxication, Westitis, and Westafflictedness. 'Occida-
tion'[1] is another interesting candidate. The major
difficulty is the lack of a verbal form in English
with the same semantic latitude and morphological
flexibility as the Persian participle __zadeh,__ which
carries the meanings of being struck, smitten, in-
capacitated, stupefied, sabotaged, diseased, in-
fested, and infatuated, all at once. The English
verbal form used to match the adjectival participle,
assuming the term is to have morphological equiv-
alence, must then be nominalized with either 'tion'
or 'ness'. 'Westafflictedness' works in some ways

(as in the pattern of 'narrowmindedness'), but it
fails to carry the feeling of a blow as directly as
does 'struck'. 'Weststruckness' carries nothing of
the Persian term's sense of disease and contagion and
the consonant sequence -stst- is not something that
would normally occur in English. 'Westoxication' is
palatable and clear, but misses both the disease and
contagion in the Persian and the sense of a blow.
The same can be said of 'Westmania'. 'Plagued by the
West' and 'Blighted by the West' are very far from
the morphological structure of the Persian (not
necessarily a serious problem in itself) and still
miss the connotations of infatuation and being
struck. There are three essential elements of meaning to be conveyed here: being smitten, being infatuated, and being diseased. No English translation
we are aware of really catches more than two of them.
We have therefore decided to retain the Persian term
throughout the text in all but a few cases.

Although Gharbzadegi has gone through numerous
editions both within and outside of Iràn, we have
seen only two major variants, the original 1962 edition, with deletions, and the unexpurgated revised
edition of 1964, which remained largely unknown until
1978. The 1962 censored edition is the one most
Iranians know,[10] and is the one which had the
greatest impact under the Pahlavi regime. Interest-
ingly, although the entire volume was suppressed by
the government during the lifetime of its author,
even the versions published abroad appear to have
been censored. Without further evidence than the
texts themselves, we can only surmise that either the
government censored Gharbzadegi and then decided to
ban it anyway, after which the censored version some-
how got out of the country, or that the groups who
undertook to publish it were themselves responsible
for the censorship. Arguments can be made for either
hypothesis, and both may be correct. The 1964
revised version was published in Tehran in 1978 by
Ravaq publishers of Tehran. It contains both the
previously censored portions and the 1964 changes
made by Al-e Ahmad. It is not always possible to be
certain whether the new elements in the Ravaq edition
were added in 1964 or censored in 1962, but some
points to bear in mind are that (1) any new text containing dated material after 1962 is obviously a
later addition by the author, (2) material on certain
subjects that appears throughout the new text and
nowhere in the early text was probably censored out
of the early edition, and (3) most of the new

parenthetical insertions were probably added later by the author as afterthoughts. We have used the following conventions to distinguish between the various categories of text: material /between slashes/ is found only in the early editions; material *in italics* is found only in the new editions; the normal font is used for text that appears in both editions; material [in brackets] has been added by the translators; the author's footnotes are followed by '(A)', and translators' footnotes are followed by '(tr)'.

The transliteration system we have used is adapted from the one proposed by Naser Sharify in his Cataloging of Persian Works (Chicago: American Library Association, 1959). All diacritics have been omitted, leaving us without a distinction in pronunciation between the long and short *a* and also ignoring a number of orthographic distinctions. The names of authors of books have been cited as they are listed by the Library of Congress, except when we have been unable to trace them, in which case they are transliterated. Our authority for place names in Iran and elsewhere is The Times Atlas of the World. Foreign terms which have come into English usage are spelled as they appear in Webster's Third New International Dictionary. Dates are given in both the Hejri and Christian Era calendars if this has been done in the Persian text or if the Persian contains only the Hejri date. For certain dates of key historical importance to Iranians (such as the fifteenth of Khordad) we have kept the month and day of the Iranian calendar in the text.

John Green
Ann Arbor, Michigan

October, 1982

INTRODUCTORY NOTES

[1]There is not much in the way of biographical
information on Al-e Ahmad in English. A good synop-
sis of the milestones of his career and a
bibliography of published works has been written by
Michael Hillmann in Major Voices in Contemporary Persian Literature--Literature East and West 20(1976):
61-64. See also the preface to Iranian Society: An
Anthology of Writings by Jalal Al-e Ahmad, compiled
and edited by Michael C. Hillmann, (Lexington: Mazda,
1982), as well as Al-e Ahmad's own brief
autobiography translated in that volume, and En-
cyclopaedia of Islam: New Edition, Supplement 1
(1980): 60-61.

[2]For a more detailed discussion of economic
policy during this period see Nikkie R. Keddie, "Oil,
Economic Policy, and Social Change in Iran," in Iran:
Religion, Politics and Society, Collected Essays
(London: Cass, 1980), which has been used for this
introductory discussion.

[3]Illich has also lived longer. He was born in
Vienna in 1926, three years after Al-e Ahmad, and is
still living today. Some of his most important books
are Deschooling Society (N.Y.: Harper and Row, 1971),
Tools for Conviviality (N.Y.: Harper and Row, 1973),
The Right to Useful Employment and its Professional
Enemies (London and Melbourne: Marion Boyars, 1976),
and more recently, Toward a History of Needs (N.Y.:
Pantheon, 1978), and Shadow Work (Boston and London:
Marion Boyars, 1981). A dated but still useful sum-
mary of his ideas and bibliography is in John Ohliger
and Coleen McCarthy, Lifelong Learning or Lifelong
Schooling? A Tentative View of the Ideas of Ivan Il-
lich with a Quotational Bibliography, (Syracuse,
N.Y.: Syracuse University, 1971).

[4]This assessment is made by Mangol Bayat-
Phillip in "Tradition and Change in Iranian Socio-
Religious Thought," Michael E. Bonine and Nikkie
R. Keddie, eds., Continuity and Change in Modern Iran
(Albany: State University of New York, 1981),
pp. 35-56. The supporting citations from Al-e Ah-
mad's travel diary used there are drawn from early
stages of the journey when the author was undergoing

a painful self-examination in an effort to rediscover his faith. Had the citations been selected from other pages where Jalal had resolved some of his doubts, the opposite view could have been supported. This article does give an important assessment of Al-e Ahmad's historical place among Iranian intellectuals. See also "First Day in Mecca," our translation of the section which is the emotional high point of Al-e Ahmad's Mecca pilgrimage, in Iranian Society, pp. 122-133, and also the remarks quoted from Simin Daneshvar, Al-e Ahmad's wife, on p. xi of the same volume.

⁵By "the Persian press" we mean the Tehran dailies Ettela'at, Sobh-e Azadegan, Keyhan, and Jomhuri-ye Eslami, all of which are subject to state control and must therefore be read more as forums for the expression of ideals and goals than as sources of reliable factual information.

⁶In an article published in the newspaper Keyhan in July of 1982, Mohammad Taqi-Banki, Minister of State, summed up the current official policy on planning as follows:

"In planning for the next five or ten years we must abandon mental patterns, and we certainly must not pay much attention to the standards in books from the East and West, despite all the research they have done. We must be thinking about plans that are in accordance with our needs, resources, and limitations."

⁷Three of these studies have appeared as separate volumes in Persian. They are Owrazan: Vaz'-e Mahal, Adab va Rosum, Folklowr, Lahjeh [Owrazan: the state of a community, manners and customs, folklore, dialect], Tehran, Ravaq, 1978, Jazireh-ye Kharg, Dor-e Yatim-e Khalij [Khark Island, orphan pearl of the Gulf], Tehran, Amir Kabir, 1352 (1973), and Tat Nishinha-ye Boluk-e Zahra [The Tati speakers of Boluk-e Zahra], Tehran, Amir Kabir, 1352 (1973).

⁸See Adamiyat's pamphlet, Ashoftegi dar Fekr-e Tarikhi [Confusion in historical thinking], (Tehran: Khordad, 1360 [May 22-June 21 1981]).

⁹Suggested by John Lawler of the University of Michigan Department of Linguistics.

¹⁰For this version of Gharbzadegi we have used

an edition published by the Muslim Students' Association in Solon, Ohio. It was printed in 1979, a year
after the unexpurgated edition has already appeared
in Iran.

GHARBZADEGI
[WESTSTRUCKNESS]

PUBLISHER'S NOTE

Readers of this text will note that the author's citations of individuals and figures are citations that were made sixteen years ago.

The author made his last revision of this text in 1344 [1964].

BY WAY OF INTRODUCTION

Sixteen Tons

I was born one mornin' when the sun didn't shine

I picked up my shovel and went to the mine

I loaded sixteen tons of number 9 coal

The small boss said 'praise God! I like it!'

You load sixteen tons and what do you get

Another day older and up to your neck in debt until
you die

Oh St. Peter! Don't call my soul

We gave our soul to the company store

When you see me comin' you'd better step aside

Many didn't do this and died

I've got one fist of iron and the other one's steel

If the right fist don't get you the left one will

Some think a human being is made out of clay

But a poor man's also a lunatic

Made of muscle and blood

With a mind that's weak and a back that's strong

You load sixteen tons and what do you get

Another day older and until you die deeper in debt

Oh St. Peter! Don't call me to die

We gave our soul to the company store

Lyrics: Merle Travis

Sung by Ernie Ford.

From a Capitol Records of America long-playing record.   (Thanks to Betty Tavakolli who transcribed the lyrics for me.) [1]

NOTE

[1]The author has taken some liberties with the lyrics to 'Sixteen Tons' in his Farsi translation, probably because he felt it necessary to make certain additions and changes to get the idea across to Iranian readers. We have retranslated the Farsi here, since the actual lyrics to 'Sixteen Tons' are known to most English-speaking readers. (tr)

FOREWORD

        The initial draft of what you will see in
this booklet is a report that was submitted to the
Commission on the Goals of the Iranian Ministry of
Education during two of that commission's many ses-
sions, on Wednesday the eighth of Azar 1340 [29 Nov
1961] and Wednesday the twenty-eighth of Dey 1340 [18
Jan 1962]. The assembled reports of that commission's members were published in Bahman of 1340 [21
Jan-20 Feb 1962] by the Ministry of Education. But
of course this report had no place among those pages,
which had no such possibility or merit. The time has
not yet come when a department in the Ministry of
Education can officially publish such a report, although the time had come when the respected members
of that commission were able to tolerate listening to
it.

This report had to remain unpublished, and typewritten copies of it fell into the hands of this friend and that benefactor, who read through it very carefully and adorned it with their comments in the margins. Among these distinguished people was Dr. Mahmud Houman, who heartily encouraged me to read the German writer Ernst Junger's work entitled Crossing the Line,² which is about nihilism, because according to him we had both observed just about the same phenomenon, but with two sets of eyes, and we had described the same phenomenon, but in two different languages. Since I didn't know German I relied on him personally. For three whole months, at least two days a week and three hours a day, I took advantage of his presence and became his student. The result was the translation of Crossing the Line through his oral interpretation and my writing.

It was at this juncture that *Keyhan's* **Ketab-e Mah** got started, *in early 1341 [21 Mar 1962-20 Mar 1963]* containing the first chapter of Crossing the Line and the initial third of Gharbzadegi [Weststruckness]. This very initial third caused **Ketab-e Mah** to be banned. Ultimately they ended up spitting out the seed of Gharbzadegi and becoming **Keyhan-e Mah**, *which itself lasted no longer than a single issue.*

As for the text of Gharbzadegi, *I published one thousand copies of it in Mehr of 1341 [23 Sep-22 Oct 1962]... independently. And now here's the same text with additions and deletions and with a revision of the injunctions and assessments.*

Let me say here that I got the expression 'Gharbzadegi' *from oral remarks made by another of my benefactors, Mr. Ahmad Fardid, who was a participant on the Commission on the Goals of the Iranian Ministry of Education. If there was give-and-take at those meetings, some of it was between him and me-- and he has more things to say on the same subject that are well worth hearing--and I was hoping that this writer's audacity would provoke him to speak out.*

The text of this second edition is somewhat more detailed than the first. I wrote it towards the end of 1342 [early 1964] for a second pocket edition in a large printing. This was confiscated during the press run and the publisher--Bongah-e Javid--went bankrupt, to my own humiliation. But can one simply sit and do nothing? So once again in Farvardin [21 Mar-20 Ap 1964] of 1343 I rewrote it and sent it to Europe, intending to have it printed and distributed by the young university students living there. This didn't happen. It came back to its unfortunate owner. With all the trimming and clipping it underwent, you'll forgive me for not having the ambition to rewrite it again, for if I'd done so something different would now be before you. But during this interval the first edition was published several times clandestinely and indiscreetly in Tehran and once from a photocopy in California without the poor author's permission. And what exorbitant sums God's servants wasted buying it! And here's to the censor, who denies an author the right to publish his work and in effect gives it to others who have the nerve, find a market, and only smell the musk when the table is set. This was how there was more jeering than discussion over these inanities, and names were passed around more than the truth hit home. But there were one or two critics, from whose writing I derived counsel and took notice of the correct points, who were so late in awakening that I came to believe in the awakening [effect] of this booklet. I came to believe that these nonsensical pages, contrary to their author's expectations, still merit discussion after six or seven years. I had thought that this subject was strictly a contemporary discussion that would be dead after two years at most. But you see that the limbs still ache and the disease's ring of contagion gets wider every day. This is why I agreed again to its publication despite all the hasty judgments, assessments, and conclusions. /The complete text of Gharbzadegi is now before you./ And forgive me if the style is still crude after so much filtration. And as before, I hope you'll keep it safe from seizure by those irreligious people we have today, who are the henchmen of devils.

NOTE

¹Frankfurt am Main, 1951 (tr).

ARDESHIR
82

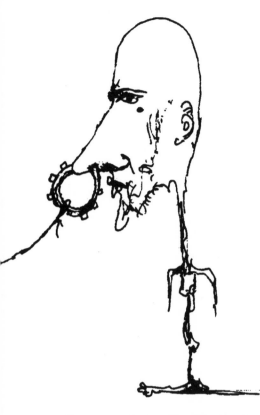

1

THE OUTLINE

OF A DISEASE

I say that <u>Gharbzadegi</u> [Weststruckness][1] is like cholera. If this seems distasteful, I could say it's like heatstroke or frostbite. But no. It's at least as bad as sawflies in the wheat fields. Have you ever seen how they infest wheat? From within. There's a healthy skin in place, but it's only a skin, just like the shell of a cicada on a tree. In any case, we're talking about a disease. A disease that comes from without, fostered in an environment made for breeding diseases. Let's look for the characteristics of this disease, its cause or causes, and if possible, a cure.

This <u>Gharbzadegi</u> has two heads. One is the West, the other is ourselves who are Weststruck. By ourselves, I mean a part of the East. Rather than two heads, let's say two poles, or two extremities, because we're talking about two ends of a single continuum, *at least, if not two sides of the world.* Instead of the West, let's say to a certain extent all

of Europe and *Soviet Russia* and all of North America,
or let's say the advanced countries, or the developed
countries, or the industrialized nations, or any
country able to bring raw materials to a state of
refinement with the aid of machines and put them on
the market as merchandise. These raw materials are
not only iron ore, petroleum, gut, cotton, or gum
tragacinth. There's also mythology. There are also
belief systems. There's also music. There are also
celestial worlds. Instead of ourselves, who are part
of the other pole, we can say Asia, Africa, or the
underdeveloped countries, or developing countries, or
nonindustrialized nations, or that group of countries
who are consumers of products manufactured in the
West, products whose raw materials--*the very ones I
listed*--come from that same part of the world, *meaning from countries in the process of growing.*
Petroleum from the shores of the Persian Gulf, jute
and spices from India, African jazz, silk and opium
from China, anthropology from the South Sea Islands,
and *sociology from Africa. These last two come from
South America too, from the Aztec and Inca tribes,
who were totally victimized by the advent of Christianity.* Yes, everything comes from somewhere, and
we're in the middle. With these latter groups our
points of commonality are more numerous than our differences.

It's not within the scope of the present work to
define these two poles or extremities from the point
of view of economics, politics, sociology, psychology, *or civilization.* Those are exacting tasks for
specialists. You will see, however, that I will be
compelled from time to time to make use of all of
these disciplines. *The only thing left to say here
is that in my view, East and West are no longer two
geographical concepts as such. To a European or an
American, the West means Europe and America and the
East means Soviet Russia, China, and the Eastern
European countries. To me, however, West and East
have neither a political nor a geographical meaning.
Instead, these are two economic concepts. The West
means the countries with full stomachs, and the East
means the ones that are hungry. To me the Union of
South Africa is a little piece of the West too, even
though it's at the southernmost extreme of Africa,
and most of the Latin American nations are part of
the East, although they're on the other side of the
globe.*

In any case it's true that to measure an

earthquake one must consult the university's seismograph, but before the seismograph records anything
the villager's horse, even though he's balky and
stupid, has fled and taken refuge in the desert. Yes,
this writer would like to sense, with a sharper nose
than a sheep dog, and with sharper eyes than a crow,
those things that others have passed over deliberate-
ly, or the presentation of which has appeared to offer no advantage to livelihood or welfare in the next
world.

Let me list, therefore, the collective general
characteristics of the countries in the first group:
high wages, low mortality rates, low birth rates,
well-organized social services, adequate nutrition
(at least 3,000 calories a day), annual per capita
income of more than 3,000 tumans [$430] per year, and
a democratic facade inherited from the French revolution.

The corresponding characteristics of the second
group are these: low wages, high mortality rates,
higher birth rates, no social services, or merely the
pretense of social services, poor nutrition (1,000
calories a day at most), annual per capita income of
less than 500 tumans [$75] per year, no concept of
democracy, and a legacy of colonization since its
earliest days. We're obviously in the second group,
*the group of hungry nations, the first group being
all the nations with full stomachs, as Josue de
Castro[2] puts it in his* The Geography of Hunger. You
see that not only is the gap between the two extremities very wide, but, as Tibor Mende said, "It is
a bottomless pit that gets deeper and deeper every
day." Thus wealth and poverty, power and impotence,
knowledge and ignorance, prosperity and desolation,
and civilization and savagery have become polarized
in the world.

One pole is controlled by *the satiated,* the rich
and powerful and the makers and exporters of manufactured goods, the other by *the hungry,* the poor and
the weak, the consumers and importers. The heartbeat
of evolution on that side of the world is progressive, while the stagnant pulse on this side is on the
verge of stopping. This disparity does not simply
arise because of the separation in space and time,
nor is it quantifiable. It's a qualitative disparity
between two widely separated and mutually repellent
poles. On the other side is a world that has become
frightened of its own dynamism, and on our side is a

world that has not yet found a channel of leadership
for its scattered movements, which dissipate instead
into nothing. Each of these two worlds is looking
for something in its own way.[3]

So the time is now past when we divided the
world into two 'blocs', the two blocs of East and
West, or communist and noncommunist. Although the
first articles of most of the constitutions of the
governments of the world still contain that huge
twentieth-century sham, the flirtation between the
United States and Soviet Russia (the two supposedly
unrivaled leaders of those blocs) over the Suez Canal
and Cuba showed how the owners of two neighboring
villages can sit down together comfortably at the
same table, and following that the nuclear test ban
treaty and other instances. Therefore our time, besides no longer being a time of confrontation between
the rich and poor classes inside borders, or a time
of nationalist revolutions, is also not a time of
confrontation between 'isms' and ideologies. Behind
the scenes at every riot, coup d'etat, or uprising in
Zanzibar, Syria, or Uruguay, one must look to see
what plot by what colonialist company or government
backing it, lies hidden. Furthermore, regional wars
of our time can no longer be called wars between dif-
fering ideas--even superficially. These days any
schoolchild not only sees the expansionist aims of
mechanized industry on both sides of the dispute at
work behind the scenes in World War II, but also sees
that the things that were happening in Cuba, the Congo, the Suez Canal, and Algeria were disputes over
sugar, diamonds, and oil. The bloodshed in Cyprus,
Zanzibar, Aden, and Vietnam was for achieving a
bridgehead to protect trade routes, which are the
first determinant of the policy of governments.

Our time is no longer a time when they scare the
people with 'communism' in the 'West' and with the
bourgeoisie and liberalism in the 'East'. Now even
the kings of nations can be superficial
revolutionaries and speak charismatically, and Khrus-
chev can buy wheat from America. Now all these
'isms' and ideologies have become pathways to the ex-
alted throne of 'machinism' and machines. The most
interesting development in this regard is the devia-
tion taken by the political compasses of leftists
and leftist pretenders throughout the world in their
turn towards the East. They have made a ninety-
degree turn from Moscow to Peking, because Russia is
no longer 'the leader of the world revolution'.

Rather it is a top contender in the circle of those
who possess atomic missiles. A direct telegraph line
operates between the Kremlin in Moscow and the White
House in Washington, showing that there is no longer
even the need for British mediation·in these dealings. Even those who hold the reins of power in our
country have realized that the danger of Soviet Russia has diminished. The pasture Soviet Russia was
grazing in was the abominable spoils of World War I.
The time has come to phase out Stalin, and Radio Moscow has come out backing the referendum of the sixth
of Bahman!ᴸ In any case Communist China has taken
Soviet Russia's place. Why? Because it is calling
all the world's underfed people to unite in the hope
of reaching paradise tomorrow, just as Russia did in
1930. If Russia had a population of some 100 million
then, China now has a population of 750 million.

It's true, as Marx said, that we now have two
worlds in dispute, but these two worlds have become
somewhat more extensive since his time, and that dispute has much more complicated characteristics than a
dispute between workers and management. Our world is
a world of confrontation between the poor and the
rich in a worldwide arena. Our time is a time of two
worlds. One is on the side of manufacturing, dis-
tributing, and exporting machines; the other is on
the side of using, wearing out, and dismantling them.
One is a producer, the other a consumer. And where
is the arena of this conflict? The world market.
And its weapons? Besides tanks, artillery, bombers,
and missile-launchers, themselves the manufactures of
that Western world, there is UNESCO [United Nations
Educational, Scientific and Cultural Organization],
FAO [United Nations Food and Agriculture Organiza-
tion], the United Nations, ECAFE [United Nations
Economic Commission for Asia and the Far East], and
other so-called international institutions that seem
to be international and universal, but the truth of
the matter is that they're Western tricksters who
bring colonialism to that second world in a new suit,
to South America, to Asia, to Africa. And this is
where the basis of the Gharbzadegi of all non-Western
nations lies. This is not a discussion about reject-
ing or refusing machines, as the utopiansᵇ imagined
in the early nineteenth century. Not at all. The
inundation of the world by machines is a historical
inevitability. It's a discussion about the nature of
our encounter with machines--as a growing nation, and
we already saw the people of the nations in the
second group--and about the fact that we don't make

machines, but because of economic and political
necessity--*and that international confrontation between rich and poor*--we must be docile and humble
consumers of Western products, or at best must be
poorly paid, contented, and submissive repairmen for
whatever comes from the West.

These things, of themselves, make it necessary
for us to adapt ourselves, our government, our culture, and our daily lives to the pattern of machines.
Everything must conform to the specifications of
machines. *If those who manufacture machines, in the
wake of the gradual changes of two to three-hundred
years, have gradually become accustomed to this new
God and its heaven and hell, what does the Kuwaiti
say, who just got his machine yesterday, or the Con-
golese, or what about me, the Iranian? How are we
going to jump out of this three-hundred-year historical pit? Forget about other people. Let me deal
with directly with us.* The basic thesis of this
short essay is that we've not been able to retain our
own *cultural/historical* personality during our encounter with machines and in the face of their inevitable assault. In fact, we've been destroyed. [6]
The point is that we've been unable to take a calcu-
lated and well-assessed position in the face of this
monster of the new century, not even to the extent
that Japan has done. The point is that as long as we
don't perceive the nature and philosophical basis of
Western culture, and continue to behave as Westerners
superficially, we'll be like the donkey who posed as
a lion and ended up being eaten by one. If the one
who builds machines is now screaming and suffocating,
we don't even complain about having become slaves to
machines. We even brag about it. For two-hundred
years we've been like a crow who tries to be a
partridge (if we can be sure which is the crow and
which is the partridge).

An obvious principle emerges from all this. It's
obvious that as long as we only use machines and
don't make them, we're Weststruck. Ironically, as
soon as we start building machines we'll be af-
flicted by them, like the West, which is now suffer-
ing from the effects of runaway technology. [7]

Never mind that we didn't even have the
capability Japan has, which undertook to understand
machines one-hundred years ago, made itself a com-
petitor with the West in its affliction with
machines, defeated the Tsars (1905) and America

(1941), and took their markets away from them before
that. The West ended up smashing them with the
atomic bomb to teach them the consequences of playing
with fire, and now *too that the Western 'free world'*
has opened the world's vast markets to Japanese
goods, *it's because they have invested in all the
Japanese industries. They also intend to recover the
military costs of protecting those islands, whose
leaders, having come to their senses since World War
II, are now totally inept where weaponry, armies, and
militarism are concerned.* And perhaps it's also because the simple American wants to ease the burden of
conscience that made a madman of that abominable
bomber' pilot who repeated the story of Ad and
Thamud' at Hiroshima *and Nagasaki.*

Something else is obvious to us as well, and *Very
well
Said*
that is that since the time the 'West' called us--
*from the Eastern shores of the Mediterranean to
India*--the 'East' as it arose from its hibernation of
the Dark Ages seeking the sunlight, *and spices, silk,
and other goods,* they've been coming to the East,
first as pilgrims to the holy shrines (*to Bethlehem,
Nazareth, and so on*), then in the armor of the
Crusades, then in the guise of tradesmen, then under
the protection of their treasure-laden warships, then
as Christian missionaries, and finally in the name of
promoting civilization. This last one was a
veritable celestial mission. After all, 'colonization' draws its roots from 'development', and whoever
engages in 'development' inevitably takes part in
civilization.

It's interesting that among those countries who
were beneath the heel of the colonialist *vanguard,*
Africa was the most receptive and promising, and do
you know why it was more promising? Because besides
the raw materials it had (*and abundant they were:
gold, diamonds, copper, ivory, and many other raw
materials*), its natives walked in no urban tradition
or widespread religion. *Every tribe had its own god,
chief, customs, and language. And so scattered! And
inevitably, so receptive to authority! Most important of all,* all its natives went around naked. *It
was too hot to wear clothes.* They celebrated *and
prayed* in Manchester when Stanley, a world traveler
in the tradition of the English humanitarian, brought
this good news back to his country from the Congo.
After all, a meter of cloth every year for every man
and woman of the Congo to put on, *become 'civilized',
and* wear to Sunday services would equal 320 million

yards of Manchester cloth every year.[10] We know that
the colonialist vanguard included Christian missionaries, and that they built churches in the
vicinity of every merchant throughout the world and,
by means of subtle trickery, persuaded the native
people to attend them. *And now, with the removal of
the feast of colonialism from those areas, for every
commercial outlet that closes, a church door closes
too.*

Africa was also more promising and receptive *for
those gentlemen* because the African natives were raw
material themselves for the use of all kinds of
Western laboratories in the development of the fields
of anthropology, sociology, ethnology, linguistics,
and a thousand other kinds of 'ologies' based on the
background of African *and Australian* experience, *ena-
bling the professors of Cambridge, the Sorbonne, and
Leiden to become established in their chairs using
these same 'ologies', and to see the other side of
their own urban civilization in African primitivity.*

We *Middle Easterners* were neither so receptive
nor so promising. *Why? Because if we want to speak
more personally, that is, to speak of ourselves, we
must ask why weren't we Muslim Easterners more receptive? You can see that the answer is embedded in the
very question,* for within our Islamic totality we apparently weren't worth studying.

It was for this reason that the West, in its encounter with us, not only came into conflict with our
Islamic totality (in the instances of the bloody encouragement of Shi'ism at the beginning of the
Safavid dynasty, *the sowing of conflict between us
and* the Ottomans, the encouragement of the Bahai
movement in the middle of the Qajar dynasty, *the par-
celing of the Ottoman Empire after World War I, and
finally in confrontation with the Shi'i clergy in the
disturbances of the Constitutional Revolution and
afterwards),* but it also tried to disrupt that fragmented totality, which was only a totality in appearance, from within as quickly as possible. They
also tried to make us into raw material like the
African natives, and then to take us to their
laboratories. *This is why the <u>Encyclopedia of Islam</u>
is at the top of the list of Western encyclopedias.
We ourselves are still asleep, but the Westerner has
taken us to his laboratory in this encyclopedia.*

India, after all, was a place something like

Geography
13 so
important

*Africa, with that 'Babel' of tongues and the disper-
sion of races and sects. And Sóuth America had in-
stantly turned Christian at the points of the
Spaniards' swords. And the Pacific was itself an ar-
chipelago of islands, which is to say the ideal setting for sowing discord. Thus, in appearance and in
the reality of the Islamic totality, we were the only
barrier to the spread (colonialism = Christianity) of
European civilization, meaning to Western industry's
search for markets.*

*The Ottoman artillery that stopped at the gates
of Vienna was the end of a process that had begun in
732 A.D. in Andalusia.*[11] *What do we call this
twelve-century period of conflict and rivalry between
East and West if we don't call it a conflict between
Islam and Christianity? In any case, now--in this
age we're living in--I as an Asian descendant of that
Islamic totality, and that African or Australian descendant of savagery and primitivity--both equally
and to the same extent--are perfectly welcome from
the standpoint of the civilized nations(!) of the
West and the machine builders to content ourselves
with being museum exhibits, to remain simply something worth studying in a museum or a laboratory and
nothing more. Don't you dare tamper with this raw
material!*

*Now it's no longer a matter of them wanting the
petroleum from Khuzestan or Qatar in unrefined form,
the diamonds from Katanga in the rough, or the
chromite from Kerman unsmelted. What matters now is
that I, as an Asian or an African, must even preserve
my literature, my culture, my music, my religion, and
everything else I have in perfect condition just like
an artifact right out of the ground, so that these
gentlemen can come and gawk, and take it to their
museums and say, "Oh yes, here's another form of
primitivity!"*[12]

*Now, after this introduction, allow me, an
Easterner with his feet planted firmly in tradition,
eager to make a two- or three-hundred-year leap and
obliged to make up for so much anxiety and strag-
gling, and sitting in the middle of that fragmented
Islamic totality, to offer the following definition
of* Gharbzadegi:

*[It is] all the symptoms that have been created
in the life, culture, civilization, and manner of
thinking of the peoples on this side of the world*

without any historical background or support from
tradition, *and with no thread of continuity through
the changes*. They are merely the by-products of
machines, or, better yet, they are their preliminary
substitutes. Having said this, it is clear that *if
it be said that we are one of those peoples, since
the discussion in this booklet in a primary way per-
tains to the regional environment, language, tradition, and religion of its author*, it is also even
clearer that if we have machines, that is to say if
we build machines, there is no further need for their
by-products to serve as preliminaries and substitutes.

Gharbzadegi is therefore a characteristic of an
era in which we haven't yet obtained machines and
don't understand the mysteries of their structure and
construction.

Gharbzadegi is a characteristic of a period of
time when we have not become familiar with the prere-
quisites for machines--meaning the new sciences and
technology.

Gharbzadegi is a characteristic of a time in our
history when we're compelled to use machines because
of the market and economic constraints on us to use
machines *and because of the incoming and outgoing
petroleum*.

What brought on this era? What happened that
other people, ignoring us completely while they
changed and developed their machines, built, carried
out plans, and moved in and out of our midst *and we
awoke to find every oil derrick a spike impaling the
land?* Why did we end up Weststruck?

Let's go back to history.

NOTES

[1] I borrowed this term from Mr. Ahmad Fardid. He's written several other things and given some talks under the same title which are most readable. It is the hope of this writer that he will be encouraged to continue discussing this matter. (A)

[2] Josue de Castro, The Geography of Hunger (Boston: 1952). (tr)

[3] *Freely translated from* Jahani Miyan-e Tars va Omid [A world in the midst of fear and hope], by Tibor Mende, translated by Khalil Maleki, Tehran, 1339 [21 Mar 1960-20 Mar 1961] (A) [Translators' note: Mende, Tibor, Reflexions sur l'histoire d'aujourd'hui, entre la peur et l'espoir (Paris: 1967)]

[4] The referendum took place on January 26, 1963. Its purpose was to produce a show of popular support for the Shah's land reform bill, which was designed to break up big estates and distribute land to peasants, and also for a law giving Iranian workers a twenty percent share of the net profits of their factories. The election, called by the Shah to bypass the National Assembly, which normally approved his decrees, marked the first time women were permitted to vote in Iranian history. It was vigorously opposed by the Muslim clergy, the National Front, the communists, and the major landowners, all of whom boycotted the polls. (tr)

[5] Referring to the spate of utopian movements that flourished in the United States in the early nineteenth century--the Rappites, the Oneida Community, the Shakers, New Harmony Indiana, and Brook Farm--to name some of the most prominent, all of whom were threatened by the disruptions of industrialization and hoped to form ideal, self-contained communities. (tr)

[6] I gave a perfect example of this in Jazireh-ye Khark, Dor-e Yatim-e Khalij [Khark Island, orphan pearl of the Persian Gulf] (Tehran: Entesharat-e Danesh). (A)

[7]See La France contre les robots (Paris: 1955), by Georges Bernanos, a contemporary French writer. (A)

[8]This pilot's name was Claude Eatherly. See the book below, which is his correspondence with an Austrian writer with an introduction by Bertrand Russell. This book was translated in Ferdawsi magazine in a series of issues in 1342 [21 Mar 1963-20 Mar 1964] by Iraj Qarib under the title "The Demolition of Hiroshima." Avoir detruit Hiroshima, ed., Robert Laffont, Paris. (A) [Translators' note: As a point of fact, Claude Eatherly was not the pilot of the aircraft that was used to drop an atomic bomb on Hiroshima. Major Eatherly piloted a plane called the Straight Flush, which overflew Hiroshima prior to the actual bombing on the same day. The Enola Gay, which actually was used to bomb the city, was piloted by Colonel Paul Tibbets. See Claude Eatherly, Burning Conscience; the Case of the Hiroshima Pilot, Claude Eatherly, Told in His Letters to Gunther Anders (New York: 1962).]

[9]Ad and Thamud were two ancient tribes said to have been among the first peoples to inhabit the Arabian peninsula. They were destroyed en masse by God (according to accounts given in the Qur'an) for disobeying their prophets. See R.A. Nicholson, A Literary History of the Arabs (Cambridge: 1956), pp. 1-3. (tr)

[10]Du Zambese au Tanganika, 1858-1972, by Livingston and Stanley (Paris: 1958). (A)

[11]I'm referring to the defeat of 'Abdol Rahman Amavi (one of the Andalusian Islamic caliphs) by the French General Charles Martel at Poitiers and the stopping of the expansion of the Western Islamic caliphate in the beginning of the eighth century A.D. And you'll remember that this 'Martel' is today the name of a famous cognac! (A) [Translators' note: This Andalusian caliph is known in Western literature as 'Abd al-Rahman B. 'Abd Allah al-Ghafiki, governor of Spain, who was killed along with most of his army by Charles Martel between the cities of Tours and Poitiers at a battleground known to Arabs as Balat al-Shuhada' (Pavement of the Martyrs).]

[12]Mr. Semin Baghchehban, a musician friend of mine, has some notes (unpublished) concerning the Music Congress of Farvardin of 1340 [21 Mar-20 Ap

1961] *in Tehran.* *There he writes: "For* [Alain] *Danielou (the French representative) nothing is more interesting than the fact that we lived during the age of the Sassanian kings and are available for him, who arrived in the heart of the twentieth century, to study, so that he, with his precise instruments and the latest tape-recording systems, can find his way to the Sassanian court, record a concert by Barbad and Nakisa, and then return to Paris on an Air France jet from an airstrip near the Sassanian capital built especially for orientalists and experts on poetry, painting, and music."* (A) [Translators' note: Barbad was a famous vocalist and lutist, Nakisa a harp player. Both were prominent entertainers in the Sassanian court of Khosraw II at the turn of the sixth century A.D.]

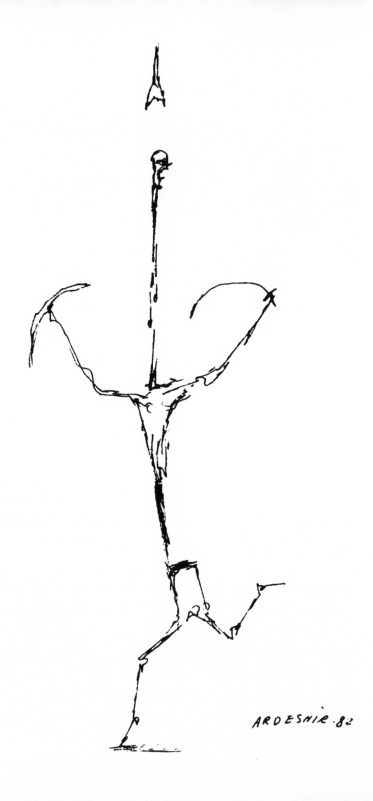

2

THE FIRST ROOTS OF
THE SICKNESS

As history shows, we have always looked to the West. We even introduced the term 'Western' before the Europeans called us 'Eastern' with the name Ibn Batutah the Maghrebi [The Moroccan],[1] or before that in the name of Gibraltar, which we knew as the farthest extremity of the *Islamic* West.

From the dawn of Islamic civilization to the collapse of every value orientation in the face of technology, on this side of the world we've always interpreted and branded the rest of the world according to our system of values, in our position as a microcosm of a larger culture, even before other people did the same thing to us. *Aren't there two sides to every coin?* If we go back one or two millenia to take a more complete look around--it was right here in this area--*in the Middle East(!)*--where the Chaldeans, the Assyrians, Elam, Egypt, the Jews, Buddha, and Zoroaster arose, on the flat expanse between the Sind and Nile valleys, *and became the*

founders of that thing, the exception of which
there's nothing at all to be found in the satchel of
Western civilization. Except for boastfulness and
conceit, of course.

This 'us', with its several dimensions,
throughout all these ages, before looking at the Far
East (*China, Indochina, and India*), *where it got*
chinaware, printing, the korsi,[2] *Sufism, painting,*
self-mortification (Jhoki practices), meditation (Zen
practices), saffron, spices, samanu,[3] *and so on,* was
already looking at the West, at the shores of the
Mediterranean, at Greece, at the Nile Valley, at
Lydia (*the center of present-day Turkey*), at
northwest Africa, and at the amber-laden North Sea.
As residents of the Iranian plateau, we were also
part of this entirety, and we were similar to it.
Why? *Let's try to find an answer by hypothesiz-*
ing. You can see that I have tightened the circle.
Now we're talking about us Iranians.

It could have been our flight from Mother
India--the first cause of our looking to the West. *A*
flight from the center? I don't know. The eth-
nologists, Aryanists, and Indo-European linguists
will have to answer that. I'm guessing. In any
case, there's no doubt about what a warm embrace
this very mother *had ready for us* in our time of
need. This same India at one time gave shelter to
the remnants of the Zoroastrians, who were too muleheaded even to pay the Islamic jaziyeh,[4] *and*
uprooted themselves lock, stock, and barrel to take
refuge in India. Today we have the Parsis of India,
their descendants, who contributed in a nasty way to
British oppression during the years of colonization,
and who now have India's industrial aristocracy in
their clutches the same way. She gave shelter again
in the time of the Mongol *invasion,* and most recently, at the point of the prejudice-drawn swords of the
Safavid Sufi pretenders. These last two times, great
treasures of thought remained untouched in India, as
she protected many intellectual resources from the
ravages of time. Although this warm embrace was always a place of refuge for us as homeless children,
no child has ever gotten anywhere under the indulgent
protection of his mother. "A spoiled child can't
make friends," as they say. By the same token, Islam
got nowhere in Mecca and Medina. It was in Baghdad,
Cairo, Seville, and Andalusia that it laid down a
glorious foundation worthy of an empire, and Christianity, which promised of 'The Great One' *and of*

Nazareth, raised its banner right in the heart of the
pagan world in Rome. Manichaeism, which arose in
Ctesiphon [southern Babylon], disappeared in Turfan
[Chinese Turkistan]. Buddhism, which was planted in
India, sprouted in the land of the Rising Sun
[Japan]. We also, when we fled from India (*if that's
what we did*), or turned our backs on it, looked to
the West. And although we had maintained friendly
relations with this *probable* mother [India], through
the comings and goings of Bozorgmehr,[5] the wander-
ings of the Sufis, our pilgrimages to Ceylon, our encounters with enemies in the wars waged by the accursed Sultan Mahmud [Ghaznavi], and the violent encounters through the raids of **Nadir** Shah the Hide-
Wearer, in all this commerce with India it was never
our objective to be close. We've never acknowledged
the bonds of relationship. I think that in all
probability one of the major causes of this thing I
call **Gharbzadegi** was our very flight from the center,
which was also a flight from hot weather. /It was as
if we'd disobeyed our parents, been cursed by them,
and had cut the ties of blood relationship and
tradition./

   Perhaps we also always looked to the West because the desert nomads of the East always drove us
in that direction, even as the Aryans drove the
demons of the **Shahnameh**[6] out of Mazandaran to the
shores of the Persian Gulf when they came. From the
Turanians of the **Shahnameh** and the Hurrians on, every
few decades a tribe, *whether Turkish or Persian-
speaking*, would migrate in search of pasture. They
swarmed in this direction, seeking an alternative to
chronic drought conditions that had suddenly over-
taken them again in those vast and distant desert
lands. Cyrus [the Great] also died in those distant
deserts in search of the Massagetae. The Ghaznavids,
the Seljuqs, and the Mongols also came *riding through
from the same deserts, and Siyavash's blood was
spilled in those deserts by Afrasiyab.*[7] There's no
century in our history that wasn't marked once or
twice by the hoofprints of the Eastern tribes. All
the dynasties of the Islamic period, with one or two
exceptions, were established by these very tribal
barbarians, *and even before Islam. Who do you think
the Parthians are?* Those who unrolled the scroll of
our history were certainly tribes, not dynasties.
Whenever we built a house, just as we were about to
apply the finishing touches to the roof, a hungry,
marauding tribe came from the East. Not only did
they pull the ladder out from under our feet, they

also demolished everything from the foundation up. On this wide racetrack which is the Iranian plateau, our cities were always pieces on a broad chessboard, like polo balls before the famine-starved desert nomad horsemen, which they picked up in one place and put down in another.*

The Soltaniyeh* domes, with all their architectural splendor and monstrous dimensions, have smiled hundreds of times with hundreds of cracks on this kaleidoscopic land. On this flat plain, only a limited number of our cities have had an opportunity to achieve greatness in their youth, to reach maturity, to stop growing in their old age, to begin to decay, and like Baghdad, which arose out of the ruins of Ctesiphon, to throw themselves like the phoenix into the fire, the source of rebirth and beauty. *This is how we've entered into a 'this too will pass' state of mind, the stone of 'each one has his allotted few days to live' has sunk to the core of our being, and 'whoever came built a new building' has become our slogan.*

Perhaps it may be said then that we've had little experience as an urban civilization and have not yet arrived at urbanization and urban (bourgeois) civilization in the true sense. And if you look at the situation today--when the stress of machine pressure is forcing us to adapt to urban civilization *and its requirements*--since this is a rapid process in itself but very late in beginning, it necessarily takes on a cancerous appearance. Our cities are now burgeoning everywhere like tumors, and if the roots of these tumors reach the villages and devour them, woe unto us....

With regard to the continuity of our urban civilization, you can't judge only by the historical exceptions you may find, such as Susa in the desert of Khuzestan, or Esfahan, Kashan, and Ray in the central deserts. The edifice of our history is not supported by foundations, pillars, walls, houses, and bazaars, *because every dynasty that spread out and set up camp here first uprooted the previous dynasty's settlements. From the Sassanians, who wiped out what was left of the Parthians, to the Qajars,*[10] *who plastered over everything the Safavids had built, and until today, when they've built the National Bank over the Takiyeh-ye Dowlat,*[11] *put the Ministry of Finance where Karim Khan [Zand]'s sleeping quarters were, and put up schools in every corner, displacing the mosques and* <u>*emamzadehs*</u>.[12]

It surprises me that we're so shortsighted with
all these open horizons. Only during the Achamenid
and Safavid periods do you find father and son working to put up the same building. In the other
periods 'whoever came built a new building'. And
how? With materials from the buildings of the van-
quished. To the point that even yesterday they
brought the marble stones from Muslim graves in Abarqu to the Imperial Palaces of Tehran. Dig into any
corner of the country and you'll find that every
building's foundations are the gravestones of van-
quished people, and the materials in every little
bridge are stones from some ancient nearby fortress.

Therefore the edifice of our semiurbanized
civilization is not one laid out by any one person,
built up by a second, decorated by a third, expanded
by a fourth, and so on. The edifice of our so-called
urban civilization, designed to accommodate the
centralization of governments, is a building that
hangs over tent posts and travels on horseback. The
Achamenids had separate headquarters for summer and
winter, and so did the Sassanians. This is how Susa
got there, and Ectabana [Hamadan], both of them capitals. There's also Ctesiphon and Firuzabad.
Specialists in ancient history have even found a
great many similarities to tents in the roofs of the
buildings of many of our historical periods. If I
assert that this is one of the reasons the West advanced and we remained behind, I'm not too far off
the track.

You will remember that throughout our history on
this broad plain we always spent the summer nights on
the rooftops, beneath the stars. It's true that the
climate and environment surrounding us is harsh and
arid, but this harshness is due to the dryness, and
coping with it--barring floods, which are a feature
of such a climate--is not so difficult except during
the very short winter. None of our large cities has
more than three months of snow, rain, and ice during
the year. So isn't Tibor Mende[13] right when he says
that the great civilizations that have developed urban technology are only found in the colder regions
of the world between the Tropic of Cancer and the
Arctic Circle?

Of course, it's not as if we were always attacked from the northeastern deserts. There was also

Alexander, who came from the provinces of the
northwestern Iranian plateau, and there was also Islam, which came from the southwestern deserts. The
encounter with Alexander and his soldiers--in spite
of a short or a long interval of Iranianness during
the time of the rule of his [Alexander's] successors
and the first manifestation of <u>Gharbzadegi</u> in our
recorded history (the Hellenization of the Parthians)--was not an encounter with nomadic horsemen.
It was an encounter with adventurers *and mercenaries
from Mediterranean cities,* who, having been aroused
by Xenophon's <u>Anabasis,</u> came riding this way with
huge leather sacks, drooling with greed for the
mysterious wealth of the Iranian kings, the treasures
of Ectabana [Hamadan], Susa, and Persepolis.

Those first colonialists of history *since the
Phoenicians!* We know that all these people have a
fixation for building cities. If they destroyed Tyre
and Persepolis, they scattered the seeds of several
Alexandrias in the form of temporary army camps from
the Nile Delta to the mouth of the Indus River, two
of which still stand today *spread out over the land*
watching the comings and goings of parvenu nations
over the blue surface of the Mediterranean. In encounters with these mercenary soldiers, if any
plundering went on, we were the first ones to do
it.[14] For every slap in the face we received from
the northeastern desert nomads, we passed one on to
the Mediterranean coastal peoples in the West. The
burning of Persepolis was done in retaliation for the
burning of Athens.

As for Islam, it bacame Islam when it reached
the populous region between the Tigris and Euphrates
rivers. Before that it was Arab primitivity and ignorance. It had never set out to shed blood. *True,
we've heard a lot of talk about the sword of Islam,
but don't you think this sword, if it was used, was
used mostly in the West? And against the Christian
world? In any case, I think this reputation is mainly due to the conflicts between the Islamic holy wars
and the early Christian martyrs. And we know what
this Christianity did as soon as it got a foothold
somewhere! During the Spanish Inquisition, in the
brutal abuse of South and Central America, in the
subjugation of Africa, or in Southeast Asia or in the
destruction of the Khmer civilization.*[15] In any
case, the Islamic 'salaam' was the most peaceful symbol ever adopted by a world religion. Aside from the
fact that we ourselves invited Islam before it ever

came to us, though Rostam Farokhzad fought to defend
the clever Sassanians and the petrified traditions of
the Zoroastrians, when the Arabs came to Ctesiphon on
their way to plunder the royal palace *and the
Baharistan carpet*,[16] the people stood waiting for
them in the streets with bread and dates. Years
before Yazdgird [III] fled to Marv[17] Salman Farsi[18]
had fled from the village of Jay near Esfahan and
found asylum with the Islamic authorities. His role
in the formation of Islam was one of a magnitude of
importance never equalled by the [Zoroastrian]
astrologer Magis in the formation of Christianity.
Islam can never be considered a world conquerer in
the same sense as, for example, Alexander. None of
that Macedonian's mercenaries *and thugs, every one of
them an exile from his own city and homeland who had
come in this direction looking for treasure*, had the
kind of inner faith *that the primitive Arabs took to
the Jaxartes and Oxus rivers.*

    Despite what has been said up until now by cer-
tain bearded scholars, who are no better than the
upstart Shu'ubis,[19] and also despite 'Umar's book-
burning *in Rey and Alexandria*,[20] the call of Islam
was a ready answer to a call that had been silenced
by melted lead three centuries before *Islam arose on
this barren plain of monarchies* in the mouths of Mani
and Mazdak.[21] If we look at this carefully we will
see that Islam itself was a fresh call meeting the
demands of the urban peoples between the Euphrates
River and Damascus, all of whom were weary of the
long wars between Iran and Rome. Seasoned by
hardship and experience, they were ripe for recruit-
ment by any movement that would bring lasting peace
to the area. We know that the Prophet of Islam had
had commercial dealings in Damascus as a youth, *and
that he had had talks with some monk in the Damascus
monastery, and so on....* Is it possible to propagate
a religion any more simply than by saying "say there
is no god but God and prosper"? In the last
analysis, wasn't this turning to Islam also a turning
to the West? This question can be answered without
hesitation when we understand the oppression that
permeated the rigid practices of the Sassanids.

    Perhaps our attention to the West also arose
from the fact that on this flat, dry plain, we were
always waiting for the clouds of the Mediterranean.
Although the light came up in the East, for us on the
Iranian plateau the *rain* clouds have always come from
the West. We also fled the southern and northeastern

deserts because of our preoccupation with the source
of our clouds, our water, and our livelihood. This
was quite the opposite of what drew the northern
Europeans away from the cold, the humidity, and the
frost of their lands toward the south and the warm
seas, in search of sexually invigorating herbs, and
hoping to open up trade routes to Africa, India, and
America so that what took the form of *acute*
colonialism might follow them. *This two-sided ten-
sion is a perpetual element throughout the history of
human civilization. The Aryan entry into Iran was
itself one of those very conflicts from the North and
the frozen lands of Jamshid and the Aryans.*

Although it may be *somewhat* audacious of me to
say so, it is my belief that if the Russians had had
a warm-water port and had ultimately been able to
realize Peter the Great's dream, and if they had been
able, at the price of colonial plundering, to raise
salaries and provide insurance and retirement pay for
the workers of St. Petersburg and Badkubeh at the
levels of the workers in Manchester and Lyon, and if
they had not been forced to endure the ice and snow
of Siberia *or Turkey and its smooth sands*, extending
as far as the eye can see, a revolution such as the
one in 1917 would not have been laid at humanity's
feet. The export of *Russian* revolutionary *traditions*
to Africa and Southeast Asia, the most recent political development of our time, *prior to the Chinese
movements*, has within it a hope that has been gestat-
ing under suppression for years, *now stepping onto
the field in a new uniform.*

If we look again more carefully, we will find
abundant evidence of this attention to the West. It
is true that the fountain of youth was in the dark
regions of the East, but Alexander, who went looking
for it, was a Westerner, and Nizami Ganjavi, who
called him a prophet *and confused him with Dhu'l Qarneen,*[22] was one of us. The Garden of Eden is also in
the West, and amber has always come from the
Northwestern seas. Baghdad, the Mecca of the heretic
Manicheans, was at the Western. extremity of the
Iranian plateau. You've certainly heard of the black
African and Roman armies, and how they're respective-
ly associated with night and day.[23] It may have been
for this very reason that no Eastern harem was ever
without its Roman maids, who were harbingers of light
and bearers of purity and good fortune. Even in
Sufism, with all its Eaststruckness (if this expression may also be used), the West made an apostate and

a zonnar-wearer[14] of the desert-dwelling Shaikh
San'an[25] through his love for a Roman maid. Even
Nargis Khatum, mother of the Shi'ites' promised Mahdi,[26] was a maid of Roman extraction. *In any case,
many examples of this nature may be found.*

What is clear is that for us, a nation never
bound by prejudice and inexperience, the road to the
West has always been open. It was open when, like
Sa'di,[27] we went to Mecca by way of [Syrian] Tripoli,
where they put us to work digging ditches. It was
open when we went to Karbala and Najaf[28] to purify
ourselves, and it's open now as we flee to Europe to
live the good life.

All this hypothesizing aside, trafficking with
the West is a natural thing in the life of a nation
that has sought to live and learn more effectively
day by day, and to die more peacefully. There's
nothing abnormal about it. *It is commerce and trafficking with near and distant neighbors, a more extensive searching and striving among humanity's other
realms of existence.* It is strange, however, that
this attention to the West, until about three-hundred
years ago, was always one-sided, one-dimensional, and
due to one cause. It arose out of spite, envy,
jealousy, *and competition.* In this past three-
hundred years it's taken on other causes, dimensions,
and faces, the faces of sorrow, regret, and subser-
vience. Before these last three centuries we were
always jealous of the West, or we were vengeful, or
we tried to compete because of their flourishing
lands, their busy ports, their peaceful cities, and
their continuous rains. Throughout all the ages that
had passed we had considered ourselves entitled to
such blessings! We considered our customs and
beliefs to be right. We called the West infidels and
we considered them deluded. Although we gave their
learned men shelter even in the midst of Sassanian
Zoroastrian prejudice, it is clear that we judged
them according to our own values. We even went so
far at times as to give ourselves license to kill
them and steal from them. We stole whatever we could
from them on that basis.

In any case, all this competition, jealously,
and spite was acceptable for us as a means of
neutralizing the harsh and notorious policies of the
Assyrians, and of exerting our own influence on them
wherever we could. We wanted to bring cedars from
Lebanon, gold from Lydia, to bring Aristotle out of

the dark Middle Ages, and to translate and propagate
him. We wanted to adopt the military system of the
Roman legionnaires, and to learn their system of city
construction. All that this two-thousand-year commerce with the West entails--with its failures and
successes and the destructiveness on both sides,
which is itself one of the mysteries of life--has
been advantageous to both sides on the whole. No one
has lost anything. If we haven't had a friendly
relationship, we've certainly had the rivalry of two
opponents. We've given a great deal and we've
plundered even more. We gave silk and oil. We were
an access road to India and we harbored
Zoroastrianism and Mithraism. The conquest of Islam
took us all the way to Andalusia. We wore the Indian
and Khorasanian turban on the heads of our Islamic
leaders, and we made the splendor of God into a halo
and placed it around the faces of the Christian and
Muslim saints. During the last two or three centuries, however, the situation has turned around completely.

Yes, I'm talking about sorrow and regret. Now
the spirit of competition is forgotten. It's now
been replaced by a feeling of helplessness and dependence. Not only do we no longer consider ourselves deserving or right (they take away the oil as
if it belonged to them, as if we had nothing to say
about it, they run our political affairs as if we
ourselves were helpless, they've taken away our
freedom as if we didn't deserve to have it) but if we
try to explain something about ourselves in this life
or in the hereafter, we judge it by their standards,
and on the orders of their advisors and consultants.
We study the same way. We gather statistics the same
way. We do research the same way, but research is
another matter, because scholarly work has developed
international procedures, and scholarly procedures
bear the mark of no nationality. But it is interesting that we take wives just like Westerners, we claim
to be free just like them, we assess the good and bad
in the world just like them, and even our days and
nights become days and nights when they affirm it, as
if our own standards had been abolished. We quote
their sources, and we're even proud of ourselves for
being their blind progeny. Yes. Of the two old
rivals, one ultimately got the job of sweeping the
floor, while the other became the owner of the circus. And what a circus! A contemptuous circus of
boasting and conceit for the riffraff so they'll load
the oil! What's happened during these last two or

three centuries? What has taken place to turn things around this way? Let's go back to history again.

NOTES

¹Al-Maghreb, the Arabic term for Morocco, literally means 'the place in the West.' The name Maghrebi literally means 'the one from the place in the West', or 'Westerner'. (tr)

²The <u>korsi</u> is the Iranian communal heater. It consists of a low platform with a charcoal brazier beneath, covered by a blanket. Users gather around the platform and slide their legs beneath the blanket. (tr)

³<u>Samanu</u> is a dish made with the juice of germinating wheat or malt mixed with flour. (tr)

⁴Head tax on free non-Muslims under Muslim rule. (tr)

⁵Sixth century vizier under Anushirvan the Just (Khosraw Parviz). (tr)

⁶Epic Iranian poem by Firdawsi (941? - 1020 A.D.). (tr)

⁷Siyavash and Afrasiyab are both figures from the <u>Shahnameh.</u> Siyavash was a heroic figure who excelled both in bravery and purity. Afrasiyab was the evil Turanian [Turkish] king who killed him after giving the young hero refuge from his father. (tr)

⁸*It's an unacknowledged historical reality that though they've been continually trying to scare us with communism for the forty-some years since the October revolution, our urban civilization only found relief from the evils of chronic invasions by that area's desert nomads after the establishment of Soviet Russia and its republics such as Turkestan, Kergiziya, and Tajikestan. The establishment of new Soviet-style governments in these areas I've enumerated since 1917 has quieted down the bedoins and the desert nomads, and made the deserts relatively prosperous and the cities vast, with factories, farms, schools, and other urban institutions. There are no longer any tribal organizations to invade us, and if there are they no longer need to saddle up and ride 1,000 farsakhs [farsakh = 6.24 kilometers] to*

*Khorasan. They stay right there and work in the
nearest towns, villages, and farms.* In this way the
concept of tribal assaults--invasions from foreign
desert nomads from the Northeast--has lost its meaning. Since the beginning of the twentieth century it
has been replaced by the industrial assault (because
of oil) and the invasion of the 'civilized' foreigners! And that comes from the West and the Southwest. (A)

⁹The fourteenth century Mausoleum of Oljeitu,
considered one of Iran's architectural masterpieces,
located in Azarbaijan near Zanjan. (tr)

¹⁰One incident of the type referred to here was
the Qajar governor of Esfahan Mas'ud Mirza Zel os-
Soltan's decision to plaster over the mural-decorated
walls of a palace built by the Safavid Shah 'Abbas,
out of jealousy. (tr)

¹¹Takiyeh-ye Dowlat was a theatrical structure
incorporated into the Tehran Bazaar. Built in the
nineteenth century by Nasir od-Din Shah, it was
modeled after London's Albert Hall and was used as a
place for public congregation, especially for
religious gatherings and the performance of passion
plays. (tr)

¹²Emamzadehs are burial shrines containing the
remains of descendants of the Shi'i Imams. They are
highly revered in Iran and are frequently the goal of
pilgrimages. The term can also apply to the descendants themselves. (tr)

¹³See the same translated book by Tibor Mende
mentioned previously. (A)

¹⁴See the article, "Eskandar-e Gojasteh ya
Bozorg" [Alexander the Accursed or the Great] by Par-
viz Daryush in the first issue of Keyhan's Keyhan-e
Mah, Khordad, 1341 [22 May-21 June 1962]. (A)

¹⁵Regarding the Inquisition, refer to any available history of European civilization. Concerning
South America, refer to the history of the conquis-
tadors, who wiped out the Inca and Aztec civilizations as missionaries of Christian love and peace.
Concerning Africa and Southeast Asia, the latest
documentation is in Andre Gide's Return from Chad and
Andre Malraux's The Royal Road. Most important of
all is the little booklet called A discussion of Im-

perialism, by Ameh Sezar, translated by Hezar Khani, published by Nil. (A) [Translators' note: Andre Paul Guillame Gide, 1869-1951, *Le retour du Tchad, suite du voyage au Congo, carnets de route* (Paris: 1928), and Andre Malraux, *La voie royale* (Paris: 1968)]

[16]A 30 X 30-yard carpet kept in the royal palace at Ctesiphon woven from golden threads and depicting elaborate springtime landscapes. (tr)

[17]Yazdgird III was the last of the Sassanian monarchs. He fled to the city of Marv in 638 A.D. to escape the advancing Arab armies bringing Islamic rule to Iran. (tr)

[18]A legendary companion of the Prophet. Salman Farsi (or al-Farsi) was reputed to have been a slave before his conversion to Islam and to have obtained his freedom with the Prophet's help. This took place in Medina after he had spent years migrating from place to place and experimenting with various religions, including Christianity. (tr)

[19]The Shu'ubis (or Shu'ubites) were a largely Persian ninth century movement that initially proclaimed the equality of all Muslims, attacking Arab claims of racial superiority, and at times even argued later that Arabs were racially inferior to other peoples. (tr)

[20]Many Shi'i Muslims believe that 'Umar ibn al-Khattab, the second caliph, ordered his military commander, Sa'd ibn Waqqas, to burn the Zoroastrian libraries in Iran during his campaigns there. This allegation is generally disputed by Sunni Muslims, but no one has accounted for the missing books. (tr)

[21]Mani was the third century founder of Manichaeism. Mazdak was the 5th century founder of Mazdakism. Both were killed by Zoroastrian priests. (tr)

[22]Nizami Ganjavi, 1140 or 41-1202 or 3, renowned court poet, wrote one of several Persian adaptations of the *Iskandar Nameh*, a romance of Alexander the Great, ultimately derived from the pseudo-Callisthenes original in Greek, which had been translated into into Pahlavi. Dhu'l Qarneen (the one with two horns) is an individual mentioned in the Qur'an.

There is a controversy over whether the actual historical figure was Alexander the Great or the South
Arabian King Tubba' al-Akran. (tr)

²³The two Persian words used here, Rumi and Zangi, refer both to Romans and Ethiopians and to the
archetypal opposites of black and white in some
proverbs, such as "you can't wash a Zangi white,"
etc. (tr)

²⁴Christians of the Levant were required to wear
a girdle or belt called a zonnar to distinguish them
from Muslims during Attar's time. (tr)

²⁵See The Conference of the Birds, by Farid al-
din Attar, 13th cent. (New York: 1969) for the full
story of Shaikh San'an. (tr)

²⁶The Mahdi is the Twelfth or 'Hidden' Imam for
the Ithna'ashari (Twelver) Shi'is, who believe he
will reappear at the end of the Greater Occultation
to establish the true faith throughout the world and
establish a brief reign of justice before the coming
of the apocalypse. (tr)

²⁷The celebrated thirteenth century Persian poet
Sa'di was captured and enslaved in Syrian Tripoli
during one of his many extensive journeys. (tr)

²⁸The Iraqi cities of Karbala and Najaf contain
the two principal shrines of Shi'i Islam. Karbala,
some sixty miles south-southwest of Baghdad, is
celebrated because of the fact that the Prophet
Mohammad's grandson, Husayn ibn 'Ali, was killed and
his decapitated body buried there. Najaf is about
fifty miles south-southeast of Karbala. It is
revered because it contains the tomb of the Prophet's
cousin and son-in-law 'Ali, the fourth Caliph of Islam and the first Shi'i Imam. Both cities have long
been centers of opposition to the government in Baghdad, and until recently Najaf was the world center of
Shi'i religious authority. (tr)

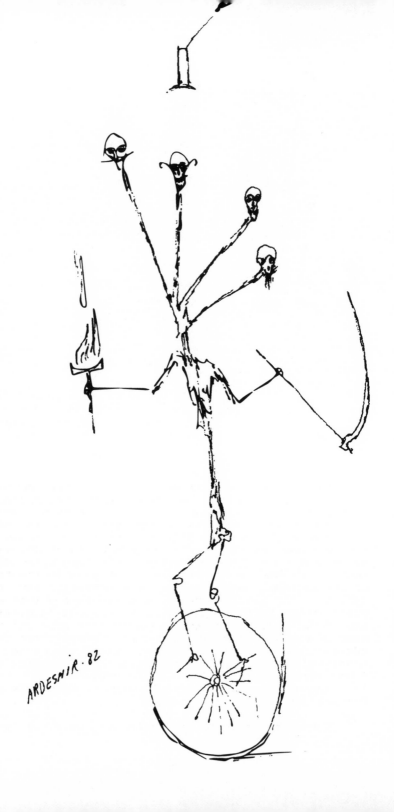

ARDESHIR.82

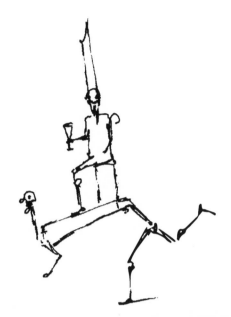

3

THE ORIGINAL SOURCE OF THE FLOOD

During the last three centuries the Western world, on the one hand, has simmered in the cauldron of the Industrial Revolution, and feudalism has given way to urbanism. On the other hand, we in this corner of the East have taken refuge in the cocoon of our unified nation built on the basis of Shi'ism. We've woven a tighter web around ourselves every day, and if we've had any uprisings, they came in the form of the Batenis, the Noqtavis, the Horufis,[1] and the Bahais. For every school and laboratory that was built in the West, we formed more secret societies and took refuge in the Seven Mysteries,[2] and the name of the Almighty. It was during these three centuries that the West ultimately, with the help of machines, underwent a monstrous transformation and found itself in need of a chaotic world market, both for the purpose of obtaining cheap raw materials and for selling industrial products.

During these three centuries, we were so busy

fighting off the Ottoman Empire that we didn't notice
what was happening. The West not only devoured the
Ottoman Empire and made its bones into cudgels for
its own protection in the event of any uprising by
the people of Iraq, Egypt, Syria, or Lebanon, but it
also came straight away after us. This is where I
see the primary sources of <u>Gharbzadegi</u>. It is to be
found on the one hand in the aggressiveness of
Western industry, and on the other hand in the impotence of our traditional national government, which
has come into power through the use of force.

Since the time our clerical establishment forgot
that it had become an instrument of government oppression, since the time Mir Damad and Majlesi[3]--at
least in their tacit approval of the Shi'i revival--
put themselves in the service of the Safavid court *by
producing made-to-order precedents in religious legal
traditions,* we, mounted on the steed of Islam, were
reduced to keeping graves and feeding on the tidbits
left to us by Shi'i martyrs. From the very day we
abandoned the possibility of becoming martyrs ourselves and contented ourselves with honoring martyrs
of the past, we became gatekeepers at the graveyard.
It's a situation I've described in <u>Nun va al-
Qalam</u>.[4],[5]

Again we see that the situation has two
aspects. Although this summary is in no way intended
to be a search for the philosophy of history, I have
no choice but to discuss these two aspects, but it is
not my task to identify the causes of the West's Industrial Revolution. The Westerners themselves have
spoken about this matter, and we, who are severely
'Weststruck', have blared this nonsense repeatedly
for years in our schools, our academies, and our
radio programs and publications: the Renaissance,
the invention of the compass, the discovery of
America, the rounding of the Cape of Good Hope, the
invention of steam power, the opening of India, the
invention of electricity, and so on. One may even
encounter these inanities in our fifth-grade elementary school geography textbooks. *Regarding this
there's one point I must refer to before going on.*

*That point is that the West--the Christian world
of the Middle Ages--when it found itself encircled to
the maximum extent possible by the Islamic world,
that is, when it was faced with the threat of
obliteration by the power of the Islamic nations from
two or three directions (from the East, the South,*

and the Southwest) and was obliged to marshall its
resources right there in those few Northern Mediterranean states, it had a rude awakening and was pushed
into a hopeless aggressive campaign against the Islamic threat, like a cat trapped in a room. When did
this happen? Towards the end of the sixth century
A.H. (twelfth century A.D.)--when the University of
Cordoba was at one end of the Islamic world in Andalusia, the Balkh and Bokhara schools were at the
other end, and all of Jerusalem, the eastern,
southern, and western shores of the Mediterranean,
and even the island of Cicily were under Muslim control. It was immediately after this that the peace-
loving Christians, who had been derisive of the Islamic holy wars were transformed into holy-war-
waging Crusaders and laid down a foundation during
the long Crusades borrowed from Islamic arts and
knowledge which transformed the Christian world after
five or six centuries into the lords of capital, the
arts, and knowledge, and after seven or eight centuries into the lords of industry, machines, and
technology. So if the Christian West suddenly awoke
with the fear of obliteration and overthrow in the
face of the Islamic danger, fortified itself, went on
the offensive, and inevitably saved itself, hasn't
the time come now for us to sense danger and
obliteration in the face of Western power and rise
up, fortify ourselves, and go on the offensive? In
the matter of our helplessness, however, there are
one or two points about which you have heard and read
less. I will discuss these points. As for the other
points, refer to the histories of civilization.

(margin handwritten note: very fine argument)

     The first point is that the Iranian plateau, un-
til prior to the discovery of sea routes, though not
the only route, was at least a passageway for the
major routes from the Far East to the Far West (from
China and India to the shores of the Mediterranean).
It was a trade route for silk, spices, paper, and
goods from China, India, and Iran /to Trebizond,
Tripoli, and Damascus/ for the Western world. It was
along the routes of these same richly laden caravans
that our major cities were built and fortified. They
were secure havens where caravans from both ends of
the world stopped to take shelter beneath those shady
arches, and in so doing breathed life into our cities
and villages. It was a road that passed through Kandahar, Herat, Tus, Neyshapur (Sad Darvazeh), Ray,
Qazvin, Tabriz, Khvoy, and Erzurum to Trebizond or
Mesopotamia or Syrian Tripoli. This was the northern
silk route. There was another route that went from

the banks of *the Indus River by sea to Hormoz, Qeshm, and then* to Kerman, Yazd, Esfahan, Varamin, Saveh, Hamadan, Kermanshah, and Mowsel until it again reached the same set of *eastern Mediterranean* ports.

With the exceptions of the fringes of Mazandaran and the plain of Khuzestan, each of which has its own separate status and story, the oldest civilizations on our plateau are in these same cities I have listed or else buried in the bellies of the huge mounds alongside them.

From the time the sea routes were opened and the seafaring community summoned the courage to penetrate to the heart of the ocean with no prospect of finding a *nearby* secure port, from then on, *besides the fact that the West acquired the new American continent, which was itself a foothold for them on that side of the world,* on this end our cities, our partially developed urban culture, and our civilization remained but an empty husk, like the empty skin shed by a snake. Only a skin. The skins of caravanserais, the skins of cities, the skins of ceremonies and culture, the skins of religion and beliefs, and the skins of our economic base. From that time on, poverty in its true sense has been with us and we've been a forgotten people in the world of the living, a graveyard of memories, keepsakes, and monuments to open roads and wealthy caravans. We were forgotten from the very time they took the shadow of their wealth out of our cities and took India and China directly to the West by sea, and we descended into the cocoon of Safavid Sufism *and the cocoon of a unified nation built on a Shi'i foundation.* The world withdrew from us and we withdrew from the world *and considered the West a defiled place. We've* discussed this deplorable matter.[6] When the two ends of the world joined hands without any need for the hospitality of our caravanserais, we became merely a nonaligned country somewhere near India--an area that was supposed to stay calm *and not rock the boat,* required only to refrain from making trouble for India or becoming the source of a threat *to the East India company. Things stayed this way and stayed and stayed and stayed until the oil monster reared its head in Khuzestan. And we again came into our own as the center of attention in the manifest world and as the basis for the struggle between East and West and the United States and England.*

In any case the study of the reasons for Middle Eastern backwardness during these last three centuries and the advancement of Westerners during the same period has not been undertaken by anyone I know of. It is now a worthy subject for investigation and study.

The second point is that the *dukes* of the Venetian Republic (the reconnaissance people for the merchant Christians or the Christian merchants) were not the first people to attach themselves to the pagan tribal peoples of northeastern Iran in their search for an ally to ward off the evil of the *Muslims*--their enemies in the crusades. The caliphs of Baghdad played this tune before them. They spread their conspiracies all the way to Qaraqorum[7] like snakes in the grass in order to quell the uprisings in Khorasan and Iraq.[8],[9]

In order to provide assistance to the various Ghuzz, Seljuq, and Mongol tribal groups and desert nomads they gave them authorization to pass through, graze their herds, and settle throughout the Eastern Islamic world. Things progressed to the point that by the end of the Samanid period all the military commanders of Khorasan, Balkh, and Iraq were all tribal chieftains, the Atabeks, the Arslans, and the Sabok-tagins.[10] In any case, if this wasn't intentional it's clear that this search for aliies during the critical confrontation with the Islamic totality had begun several years earlier with the building of the walls and towers of the merchant houses of Genoa and Venice.[11] A European writer has this to say concerning this matter:

> The historical importance of Turkish Christianity is very great. We know that the state of Sogdiana [Transoxania], which the Western Turks have inhabited since 565 A.D., was one of the largest centers of activity for the Nestorian church. It was from here and also from the state of Balkh that the Nestorian Mongols set out to convert Asia to Christianity... It appears that by around 1000 A.D. Nestorian missionaries had completed the task of converting the rear guard of the Turkish tribes in Central Asia. These tribes were the Ognigut of Inner Mongolia, the Kerait of Central Mongolia, and the Naimans of Western Mongolia. This is apart from the Uighurs who had adopted

*Christianity some time before in the Gobi
desert. In any case, the semi-Christian
face of Genghis Khan's empire can only be
explained by taking into account the Nes-
torian faith of all these Western [sic]
Turks who rode with him bearing their
swords.* [12]

It is *neither surprising* nor what I would call
an accident if we see that at this point the Islamic
world was suddenly threatened from two directions in
the seventh and eighth centuries A.H. (thirteenth
and fourteenth centuries, A.D.), by the Mongols *with
a 'semi-Christian face'* from the East and the *fully
Christian* Crusaders from the West. It was at this
point that Marco Polo and his train of litter-bearers
entered the arena.

The Europeans of the fourteenth and fifteenth
centuries A.D., who fought the Ottoman Turks,
explored the West African coast, rounded the
Cape of Good Hope, fought the Muslims in the
Indian Ocean, and mistakenly believed that
they would find their old anti-Muslim allies
on that side of the ocean--meaning the Mongol
chiefs--were all grandchildren of the war-
riors of the first crusade. [13]

/You can see that the matter is very clear./

*A third point is that the Crusaders who had
saddled up to come here and take over the Islamic
world were from all over Europe--from Sweden to
Rome--and they all had an order from the Great Pope
in hand along with money, rations, horses, and fodder
from the merchant houses of Genoa and Venice on their
backs. And which 'Islamic world' did they fight?
Not all the Islamic nations, but only the Egyptian
Mamlukes--the hand-picked distant agents of a
caliphate that was on the verge of disintegrating. I
don't think even Sa'di was volunteering to fight the
infidels when they enslaved him to dig that moat in
[Syrian] Tripoli.* In those days in this part of the
Islamic world no one was disturbed enough by the
danger to stop bickering over petty territorial
claims, or to stop talking about the revelation of
the Qur'an and its precedence long enough to strike
down the opponent. [14]

*Apart from the fact that the Mongol invasion
brought such complete waste and devastation to the*

Islamic world that nothing man-made was left standing, it was then that Marco Polo, actually representing the Pope but pretending to be on a trade mission,
traversed this entire decimated landscape talking
about the inherent ambiguities of ownership, and went
to congratulate the tribesmen who had done such a
good job of opening the way for the Venetian merchants. The most immediate result of the coming and
going of these Venetian traders was the revival of
the silk and spice routes that consequently made a
Romeo and Juliet setting of the Venetian palaces.
/The late ['Abbas] Iqbal writes,/

> As a result of the efforts of the Mongol
> tribal chiefs and the Venetian traders, two
> great routes were opened. One was the
> Greater Armenian Route (Tabriz, Khvoy, Malaz-
> girt, Erzurum, and Trebizond), the other the
> Lesser Armenian Route (Tabriz, Erzurum,
> Sivas, and Alexandretta).[15]

With the Ottoman Muslim conquest of Constantinople, however, and the decline of the Eastern
Roman Empire of Byzantium in 857 A.H. (1453 A.D.),
these newly secured routes were closed again, and
Christian Europe, accustomed to Eastern luxuries,
scrambled to find another route. As a result of this
search, first America was discovered and then the
Cape of Good Hope was rounded. Exactly fifty-three
years after the fall of Constantine and fourteen
years after the establishment of the Safavid government (891 A.H./1487 A.D.) Bartolomeu Dias passed the
Cape of Good Hope. Five years later Vasco da Gama
reached the warm seas by the same route and disem-
barked at the Indian port of Calicut. Eight years
later /the Portuguese/[Alfonso de] Albuquerque conquered the government of the Emirs of Hormoz with his
cannons and positioned himself at the mouth of the
Persian Gulf,[16] so that later he could drive the
first spike of colonialism into Goa in India, the
same one that five-hundred years later--just
recently--was pulled out of the ground.

These things are all historical realities, each
one true in its own right. Before all this, however,
the West was already contemplating other plans. The
last point I want to mention is this: If one of the
reasons for the Mongol invasion of the Islamic world
wasn't prior preparations made by Christianity in the
deep and distant deserts, at least we will find plen-
ty of evidence of instigation by Europeans frustrated

in the Crusades *and in need of the bounty of the Eastern bazaars* /in Tamerlane's invasion of this part of the world. Lest I become an example of Gharbzadegi/ I won't use European sources, *because they're careful about how they portray themselves.* Let's thumb through our own literature. We'll see their tricks and ambiguities more clearly. Ibn Khaldun, who *towards the end of his life* saw Tamerlane himself and had some discussions with him, wrote:

> While I was still in Morocco I had heard many predictions of the rise of Tamerlane. Astrologers were awaiting his appearance around the year 766 A.H./1384 A. D. One day in the Qarawiyin Mosque in Fez, I met the Constantine preacher 'Abu 'Ali b. Badis, whose opinions are reliable. I asked him about the expected [celestial] conjunction. He said, "It indicates the appearance of a powerful person from the northeastern desert peoples who will be victorious over these kings and who will take over the biggest part of the inhabited quarter of the world." Apart from him, Ibn Zarzar, the Jewish physician of the son of Alphonso, king of the "Franks," has also written the same thing.[17][18]

Notice that of the bearers of this news, one was a preacher from Constantine, which had recently been conquered by the Ottoman Muslims, and the other was a Jewish physician from the royal Frankish court. Don't you think we're right to read from this clear historical evidence that the Mongol ransacking hadn't done enough damage to Islam to suit them? And didn't they always dream in the West of the advent of another savage conquerer who would ultimately come *and drive these heroic Muslims into the ground*? If you still have doubts, note that not a spark ever landed on the Christian world, either from the withering fire of the Mongols, or from Tamerlane's massacres. And even Russia, which was chastised a little, was being punished for the sin of being 'orthodox' and yet not bowing down to the Great Pope of Rome. And if you still have doubts, note again that exactly fifty years after the Muslims conquered Constantinople, the Safavid government was established in Ardebil,[19] right behind the Ottoman Empire, the best place to stab them in the back. Don't you know that at Chaldiran,[20][21] the blood of about 500,000 Muslims was shed on both sides in domestic mass murders?

Don't think I'm defending the Ottoman Turks.
No. I want to say that it's because of this indis-
criminate regional bloodletting and the anemia it
caused that the people of the Middle East are in
their present predicament. I want to know whether
our bearded historians have the right or not to
defend that policy of stirring up religious discord.
Perhaps it's true that if the Ottomans had been victorious, or if the Safavids hadn't played a
separatist tune under the banner of Shi'ism, we'd be
a province in the Ottoman Caliphate now. Isn't it
true, however, that we're now a puppet state of the
West? Isn't it also true that for the first six or
seven centuries of the Islamic movement we were in
the same position, and while we were outwardly a
state under the Baghdad Caliphate--posing as a part
of the Islamic totality--we carried the lion's share
of the Islamic world on our shoulders? Isn't it true
that even during the darkest years of Umayyad power,
again it was we who, bolstered by nationalism and our
own original Iranian contributions to Islam, carried
the *black* Abbasid banner from Khorasan to Baghdad?
So clearly did we mark Islamic culture with Iranian
colorations and trademarks that these dilettante
orientalists are still at a loss, when they talk
about Islamic culture, *to determine what percentage
of Islamic civilization ought to be considered non-
Iranian,* [and] /to find a way to specify how any non-
Iranian elements had a hand in the building and
development of this culture/.

The point is that we must be open-minded, and
look to see what calamities have come to the East, or
to all of us the Westerners call the Middle East, as
a result of such *divisive* policies and the bloody,
interminable, and halfhearted disputes that were
stirred up with the secret help of the clergy and
with encouragement from the Christian European ambassadors who fomented discord between the Shi'is and
the Sunnis, and at the chronic anemia we've inherited
from that period. *And see how the European writer
talks of that policy of dividing and weakening the
East with such arrogance and with what barely concealed visciousness!* Yes, this very *Rene Grousset*
says:

> *This is how Iran finds its place among the
> world's large autonomous countries. The first
> reason is the court of Esfahan's relations on*

the one hand with the Mongol chieftains and on
the other with the Western powers. These relations with the West have great importance, especially from the point of view of world history,
because unlike the Ottoman Empire Iran has
turned out to be a natural ally with the Christian world. This historic mission is what led
prominent nineteenth-century European travelers
to   the   Esfahan   court--first   the Shirley
brothers--those remarkable English adventurers
who were personal friends of Shah Abbas--and
then Tavernier and Chardin....[22],[23]

     With your permission I will again quote Ibn
Khaldun so as to avoid complaining about foreigners
and all that. He says of Tamerlane, "Some consider
him a natural scholar, and others consider him a
heretic because they have seen that he regards the
family of 'Ali with preference."[24],[25] You see that
this kind of talk started long before the Safavids
appeared.   What did this 'heretic' Tamerlane do?
Once more the Islamic world was so trampled that no
trace remained of either the vine or the grower. If
Hulagu,[26] fearing the trembling of the earth and sky
and the wrath of God, wrapped the Baghdad Caliph[27] in
a carpet and smothered him to death in 657 A.H. [1218
A.D.], this second ruffian put Bayazid [I] Yildirim
(the Thunderbolt) who was the last of the Seljuq
Turks, on display in a cage[28] like a tiger just to
please the non-Muslim Christians.[29] In any case, the
eighth century A.H. [fifteenth century] feudal world
was so rife with terror, destruction, and helplessness that the Safavids didn't even have to kill
people to obtain their allegiance.

     The point of all this hair splitting is not to
go back in time to complain and moan or to suggest
that it reflects on me if Rostam was or was not a
hero in Sistan. The point is that I want to understand how the worm found its way into the tree itself
so that Sa'di could say just a year before the murder
of the Baghdad Caliph and in the height of that Mongol plundering:

At that hour when times were happy for us

When six-hundred and fifty-six years had passed

since the Hegira.

Or Ibn Khaldun, a man who walked over the entire

Western Islamic world as a judge, a minister, and a counselor to princes and wrote such a great book on the philosophy of history--how did he give in to the situation and despair so much out of weariness caused by the internal bickering of the Muslim princes in Andalusia that he was waiting for any savage conquerer to come and cut off the hand of Islam, even at the price of annihilation?

NOTES

¹Three early Shi'i 'heretic' groups. (tr)

²Referring to the seven stages of initiation, or 'valleys' in Sufism. See Attar, op. cit. (tr)

³Prominent clergymen who were politically powerful within the early eighteenth-century Safavid Shi'i government. (tr)

⁴Nun va al-Qalam [The letter 'N' and the pen] (Tehran: Amir Kabir, Aban [Oct 23 - Nov 22], 1967). (A)

⁵See also Shahrough Akhavi, Religion and Politics in Contemporary Iran (Albany, N. Y.: 1980), pp. 13-16, for elaboration of this point. (tr)

⁶We still have many of these cities. We have Bushahr, Kerman, to a certain extent Yazd, and especially Abarqu. Farrokh Ghaffari writes, in his manuscript Rahnama-ye Iran [Guide to Iran], "In the year 340 A.H.(950 A.D.) Istakhri found Abarqu to be a thriving city. Twenty-five years after him, ibn Hawqal found the bazaars of the same city flourishing. This city was located in the path of one of the trade routes of Mongol times. It went from Hormuz to Kerman, Yazd, Kashan, Soltaniyeh, and Tabriz, and from there to the Mediterranean Sea and Europe. Well-known for its spices and silk, this road connected China and India to the West. Abarqu profited by the passing of caravans. The important markets along this route were Kerman, Yazd, and Shiraz for fabrics, and Shiraz, Hormuz, and Soltaniyeh for jewelry. Hamd Allah Mustawfi saw the place in 740/1340. At the end of the fifteenth century A.D. the Portugese discovery of a sea route to India completely cut off the famous silk route. The caravanserais, homes, and mosques of Abarqu fell into total disuse, and the Afghani invasion of 1135/1735 laid such waste to the city that today Abarqu is among the most forlorn cities of this country." (A) [Translators' note: al-Istakhri, 10th cent., and Ibn Hawqal, Abu al-Qasim Muhammad, fl. 943-977, were both Arab geographers. Hamd Allah Mustawfi Qazvini, fl. 1330-1340, was a Persian his-

torian.]

⁷Now a Mongolian city in ruins, Qaraqorum was
the   thirteenth century capital of the Mongol empire.
(tr)

⁸/How well Dr. Mahmud Houman has shown this in
his manuscript Hamle-ye Ordu-ye Moghul beh Iran [The
Mongol horde's invasion of Iran]./ (A)

⁹At this point the Muslim Students' Association
edition contains these lines, which are deleted in
the Ravaq edition: /Aside from the fact that the
destruction [the Venetians] caused in the Islamic
world was definitely not the work of the chivalrous
knights of the feudalist Crusades. It was [the
result of] the mathematical foresight of the merchants of Venice and Genoa./ (tr)

¹⁰These are all well-known Turkish proper names
not necessarily intended to suggest particular individuals. A number of individuals with these names
have played important roles in Iranian history. (tr)

¹¹When the Isma'ili Shah Hassan II, Jalal od-Din
Hassan, realized that the Mongols were coming... in
his fear he sent an envoy to France to solicit help
from another People with a Book in overthrowing the
infidels. But these People with a Book weren't eager
to help. When the envoy gave up on France he put to
sea and went to England with the same message. The
envoy reached the English court in 636 A.H. [1197
A.D.]. The English historian Matthew Paris gives an
account of the envoy's unfortunate meeting with the
English king in his history. The Bishop of
Winchester, who was present at the gathering, relates
the king's vehement answer: "Let those dogs fight
and devour one another and when we go to fight the
enemies of Christianity we'll kill the survivors...."
From the article Mah va Aftab [Moon and sun] by
Mehrdad Samadi, pp. 65,66 of Ketab-e Hafteh, 14 Mehr
1342 [6 Sep 1963]. (A) [Translators' note: See Matthew Paris, 1200-1259, English History from the Year
1235 to 1273, translated from the Latin by J.A. Giles
(New York: 1968).]

¹²Rene Grousset, La face de l'Asie Ed. Payot
(Paris, 1962). (A) [Translators' note: The word
'Western' in the quotation taken from Grousset is a
significant mistranslation. The French text contains
the term 'Orientaux', or 'Oriental'.]

[13]*Tarikh-e Tamadon-e Gharb va Mabani-ye An dar Sharq* [The history of Western civilization and its foundations in the East], tr. Parviz Daryush (Tehran: Ibn-e Sina [publisher], 1338/1951), p. 133. (A)

[14]At this point the Muslim Students' Association edition contains these lines which are deleted in the Ravaq edition: /It was during such a time that Marco Polo aroused that other non-Muslim nation with the help of the non-Muslim Christians, or if not, he at least reopened the trade routes that had recently been closed by the Egyptian Mamlukes./ (tr)

[15]*Motale'ati dar Bab-e Bahrein va Jazayer va Savahel-e Khalij-e Fars* [*Studies on Bahrain and the islands and coasts of the Persian Gulf*], by 'Abbas Iqbal [1896 or 7-1955] (Tehran: 1328 [1957]), p. 50. (A)

[16]*Jazireh-ye Khark* [*Khark Island*] *by this writer. (Tehran: Danesh, Khordad 1339 [22 May-21 June 1960]), p. 50.* (A)

[17]*Ibn Khaldun va Timurlang* [Ibn Khaldun and Tamerlane], tr. Sa'id-i Nafisi, p. 57. (A)

[18]See also Walter J. Fischel, Ibn Khaldun in Egypt (Berkeley and L.A.: U. of Cal. Press, 1967), p. 56. (tr)

[19]The coronation of Shah Isma'il in Ardebil was in 907/1503, the conquering of Constantinople was in 857/1453. Notice also that "'Ozun Hassan's wife was the daughter of Kalo-Joannes, and sister of David, the last Trebizond emperor, whose name was Despina Catherine.... This woman bore 'Ozun Hassan one son and three daughters. One of these daughters, who was engaged to Sultan Haydar, named Marta... was the mother of the Safavid Shah Isma'il and the daughter of the Greek Orthodox Christian Despina Catherine.'" (from the article "'Ozun Hassan", by Dr. 'Abd al-Hoseyn Nava'i, p. 43, Mahnamah-ye Farhang, no. 4, 1341/1962, p. 43.) (A)

[20]"The revival of Iranian nationalism on the basis of Shi'ism was not only strengthened from within but also aided by the harshness of the Ottomans from without. They called Shi'ism heresy, and Sultan Salim I carried matters to the point of announcing that the killing of one Shi'i was the pious equivalent of killing seventy Christians. Based on

that very *fatva* forty thousand Shi'is·*were* massacred
in the Ottoman Empire in a few days" (From p. 112 of
the book *The Face of Asia* by Rene Grousset). He
gives three more pages of details, and let's not forget that twice that number of Sunnis were killed in
Iran. The pity is that I heard that the *Mazare'-e
Shohada'* [Martyr's Graveyard] in Ardebil, which was a
public graveyard for the heroes of the Iranian army
at Chaldiran, was destroyed awhile back, and, as
usual, they put up a 'New Foundation School' in its
place. (A)

²¹Chaldiran is the name of a plain in northwest
Azarbaijan, and the site of a decisive Ottoman victory over the Safavids in August, 1514. (tr)

²²*La face de l'Asie,* pp. 116-117. (A)

²³Anthony and Robert Shirley were military advisors to Shah 'Abbas at the turn of the sixteenth
century during Iran's war with Turkey. See also Sir
John Chardin, 1664-1677, *Travels in Persia* (London:
1927) and Jean Baptiste Tavernier, 1605-1689, *The Six
Voyages of Jean Baptiste Tavernier* (London: 1678).
(tr)

²⁴A clear indication of Shi'i leanings. (tr)

²⁵*Ibn Khaldun va Timurlang* [Ibn Khaldun and
Tamerlane]. (A)

²⁶Hulagu, 1217-1265, the Mongol conquerer who
sacked Baghdad in 1218 and put the Caliph al-Mo'tasem
to death. (tr)

²⁷/And only a year before that Sa'di had said,
"In that time when we were happy, in 656 A.H."/ (A)

²⁸Bayazid I 'Yildirim' was captured by Tamerlane
in 1402 near Angora. Some say Bayazid was not put in
a cage, but rather on a cart surrounded by an iron
grille. (tr)

²⁹This Bayazid Yildirim wrote to Shah Mansur
(brother of Shah Shuja' and the last of the Muzafar
Dynasty) that the Ottoman clergy considered war with
Tamerlane necessary and obligatory in the war with
the Christian infidels--from vol. 1 of *Monsha'at-e
Faridun Bayk* [The published works of Faridun Bayk].
(A)

ARDESHIR . 82

4

THE FIRST SIGNS OF DECAY

It is true that the medieval demon of intellectual bondage had the run of the Middle East while the
Renaissance was emerging in the West, *and the fur-
naces of religious dispute and war were burning
brightly.* As we saw in previous pages, this part of
the world was being emptied of its rich caravans and,
for this reason, was obliged to creep along in
poverty-stricken and Sufi-affected isolation. So, *as
Mr. Fardid has said,* we began right when the West
finished. When the West got up, we sat down. When
the West awoke with its Industrial Revolution, we
fell into the sleep of the Seven Sleepers of
Ephesus.[1] We experienced the seesaw effect of the
age of intellectualism begun by the West at the end
of the eighteenth century and by us in the beginning
of the twentieth century (with the advent of the Constitutional Revolution) while Europe was moving
towards socialism and orderly procedures in
economics, politics, and culture.

Flip through the pages of the travelogues of all
the people who came this way throughout the Safavid
period as tourists, merchants, diplomats, or military
advisors, and mostly Jesuits,[1] and see what encouraging and patronizing observations they made for
those colonizers. How they supported the murderous
acts of the Safavid Shah Abbas, and Sultan Husayn's[3]
utter uselessness! From then on we began to value
the approval of the Europeans observing us, who were,
in reality, the original trainers of the commanders
and political leaders we've had these last three
hundred years. All these accolades were like a spell
in the ears of a tired old caravan master, to make
him sleep peacefully and motionlessly while others
came to plunder the caravan.

These things are the basic sources of this
dangerous flood of <u>Gharbzadegi.</u> Unfortunately, our
ears are still attuned to these self-serving words of
praise from the agents of foreign ministries who come
this way every few years as orientalists, ambassadors, or advisors, and who write up hideous scrolls
when they've finished their assignments that say
"Yes, you have the head of a lion and the tail of an
elephant." I mean that since the time of Khosraw
Anushirvan, we've been suckers for praise, sadly
trying to be great. It was after this new kind of
coming and going that the Europeans became familiar
with our ways and tendencies, learned how to astonish
us, and how to give us stocks and then manipulate our
system of import duties.[4] They learned how to break
the silk monopoly belonging to the shah of that time
(*during the Safavid period*) by competing against him
on the market, and after getting a firm foothold they
learned to use the Afghani Ghilzais,[5] to take care
of that Safavid tyrant for them by gradually reducing
him to a harmless scarecrow. Then there was Nadir
Shah (1736-1747), who so foolishly assaulted India
right when the East India Company, meaning Western
colonialism, was setting up camp in south India,
diverting the attention of Muhammad Shah's government
in North India. Later came the overthrow of Nadir
Shah. There's also [the treaty of] Turkoman Chay
(1243 A.H./1828 A.D.), which was this foolish would-
be lion's last ploy. Then came the Herat War (1273
A.H./1857 A.D.) when they completely shaved off
Iran's beard and threw the corpse onto the ground.

It has been during these last fifty or sixty
years *as the spectre of petroleum has emerged* that
we've again found something in the way of a raison

d'etre due to these very preparatory maneuvers and
precedents. Now we have become so totally impotent
that our political, economic, and cultural fate has
fallen squarely into the hands of /foreign/ companies
and *Western* governments *supporting them*. Since the
time of the Constitutional Revolution, the clerical
establishment, the last bastion of defense against
the West, has withdrawn so far into its shell in the
face of the preliminary assaults of machines, so
tightly closed all doors to the outside world, and
woven such a taut cocoon around itself that it won't
emerge again until Resurrection Day. Why? Because
it lost ground step by step. That spiritual leader
who advocated a religious government based on the Islamic shari'a and was hung at the beginning of the
Constitutional movement was a symbol of what had been
lost.[6]

I agree with Dr. Tandar Kiya, who has written
that the martyred Shaykh [Fazlollah] Nuri was not
hung because of his opposition to the Constitution,
which he had initially supported himself, but rather
because of his advocacy of a government based on the
Islamic shari'a[7]--and, I might add, because of his
advocacy of the whole idea of Shi'i Islam. For the
same reason, when this man was martyred, everyone expected a fatva[8] from Najaf, just when our pioneer
Weststruck intellectuals were in their heyday, Malkum
Khan[9] the Christian and Talibuff *the Social Democrat*
of Qafqaz! In any case, since that day they've
stamped the seal of Gharbzadegi on our brows like a
fever. To me, the corpse of that great man hanging
on the gallows is like a flag they raised over this
country after two-hundred years to symbolize the as-
cendancy of Gharbzadegi.

Now, in the shadow of that flag, we're like a
nation alienated from itself, in our clothing and our
homes, our food and our literature, our publications,
and, most dangerously of all, our education. We affect Western training, we affect Western thinking,
and we follow Western procedures to solve every
problem.[10]

If the danger was breathing down our necks at
the beginning of the Constitutional Revolution, now
it's worked its way inside us--from the villager
who's fled to the city and won't ever go back because
the door-to-door barber in the village doesn't have
brilliantine in his bag, there is no cinema there and
one cannot buy a sandwich, to the fussy minister in

the national government who has trouble with his
allergie(!) whenever he's around dust, and therefore
wanders the four corners of the earth the year
around. Why did this happen?

It happened because the last two or three
generations since the Constitutional Revolution in
this land have distinguished themselves and become
teachers, writers, ministers, parliamentary representatives, and general managers. *Not a one of them
became a specialist in any art or profession.* If
they weren't reminiscing about the frivolities of
their youths in Paris, London, and Berlin, in any
case their minds were only receptive to Aqa Khan Ker-
mani's '<u>Seh</u> <u>Maktub</u>' ['Three letters'] addressed to
Jalal od-Dowleh, and to other <u>Gharbzadegis</u> of the
first days of the Constitutional Revolution, written
in the language and style of Malkum Khan, /Sayyed
Jamal [od-Din] Afghani/, Talibuff, and others.[11]

As far as this writer can see, each of these
domestic 'Montesquieus' has a different idea. Though
they may be in agreement insofar as they all vaguely
feel that the foundation of our old society and
traditions cannot stand up to the inevitable assault
of machines and technology, and they've all bought
the erroneous concept that "taking European culture
without Iranian influence"[12] should be in vogue,
apart from this totally untried prescription, every
one of them has taken a different path to find a cure
for the disease. One supported foreign influence.
Another, imitating the West, tried to emulate Luther
by giving a new life to religion through 'reform'.
Another called for Islamic unity, even as mass murders of Armenians and Kurds disgraced the Ottoman Empire throughout the world. You must excuse me for
speaking in veiled terms, because I can't be explicit
here.

What I can say is that at the beginning of the
Consititutional Revolution, *the basic reason for*[13]
the activities of this nation's leaders was that both
opponents and allies believed that "Islam/government
based on Islamic law/religion" still had the necessary social scope to be effective protection or a
barrier against the influence of machines *and the
West*. One set out to defend it, another to attack
it. As a result, a constitutional form of government
and a government based on the Islamic <u>shari'a</u> came to
be known as two contradictory concepts, one secular,
the other religious.

All those gentlemen were blowing on the flared
end of the trumpet. Yet, they were nearer than we
are chronologically to the day when the great Mirza
of Shiraz[14] destroyed the tobacco concession *to the
English Regis Company* with a simple <u>fatva</u>, *and
demonstrated what a solid rock the clergy is, and
what a threat!* Perhaps, if we had been living then
ourselves, we would have made the same errors those
two groups made and would not now be here to write
such harsh criticism. In any case, all those honest
people were unaware at the beginning of the Constitutional Revolution that the god of technology,
which had been beating the gong for private property
for several years in Europe itself from the lofty
vantage point of its stocks and banks, could no
longer tolerate any other god, and was scornful of
all traditions and 'ideologies'.

Yes, the Constitutional Revolution, as the ad-
vance guard of machines, subjugated the clerical establishment. After that, *within a period of twentyO
years* the religious schools were confined to one or
two cities. Their influence was curtailed in the
courts and official record-keeping, and the wearing
of their style of clothing was forbidden. In reaction to all this pressure, the religious establishment *not only failed to do anything, but it continued
to concern itself with the details of prayer ritual,
or with the ritual purity and uncleanness of things,
or what to do when in doubt about whether one is on
the second or the third prayer prostration!*[15] And
they took great pains to declare radio and television, which had now become so prevalent *and beyond
the power of a superhero to stop,* to be un-Islamic,
when they could have very rightfully and appropriate-
ly fought the enemy with his own weapons by resisting
the <u>Gharbzadegi</u> of official and semiofficial stations
from special stations of their own in Qom or Mashhad,
as they do in the Vatican.

Let *me say confidentially: If the clerical establishment had realized--with the belief that it
isn't necessary to obey leaders--what a precious
jewel lay hidden in the hearts of the people, like a
seed for any uprising against a government of op-
pressors and the corrupt, and if it could have shown
the people the fundamental essence of these leaders
by means of the media (newspapers, radio, television,
films, and so on) and illustrated these general principles by means of specifics, and if it could have
created a movement for its activities by making room*

[handwritten margin notes:] He does not like the religious
Stand up at the time of Const' revolution

for the international clerical establishment, it would never have had such an obsession with trivia, which produces a life wasted as an ignorant spectator.[16] As an example to illustrate what I mean, let me just discuss the schemes the National Iranian Oil Company [formerly, Anglo-Iranian Oil Company] has hatched during the past sixty years in our politics and our society, and then I'll put aside all this talk about history.

The oil concession was granted in the very first year of the twentieth century (*1901*) by the Qajar Shah to the British /priest/ *William Knox* D'Arcy[17] who sold his rights to the famous oil company. And from 1906 on we have this uproar about the Constitutional Revolution. Where was the geographical area of the agreement? In the southwestern foothills of the Bakhtiari [Zagros] Mountains. The remnants of the first oil well still remain in Masjed Solayman. Therefore the southwestern foothills of the Zagros Mountains had to be declared off-limits to the Bakhtiari tribes as a winter camping ground, so the first oil exploration parties could conveniently explore the mountains and plains around Masjed Solayman. This is why the Bakhtiari tribes[18] took to the road and conquered Tehran with the help of the Mojahedin of Tabriz and Rasht. If our Constitutional Revolution was a half-baked affair, it was because the tribal chiefs gave their support to a movement that in principle rejected tribalism. Yes. This is why we were so preoccupied with the Constitution and despotism until the beginning of the First World War. The oil companies found oil, however, and the British Admiralty, *which had officially obtained the southern oil concession*, got its *assured supply of* fuel.

You can see that I'm not writing history. I'm making inferences, and very quickly at that. Look for reasons and actual events yourselves in history.

By the year 1300 on our calendar (1920 A.D.) the war had ended, the oil companies were now victorious, the fires of the war had died down, foreign oil consumption had decreased, and oil customers had to be found in internal markets. A strong central government, therefore, had to be installed to secure all roads and remove all roadblocks so that oil tankers could easily come to Quchan, Khvoy, and Makran. It was necessary to install gas pumps in every village to compensate for the decline in foreign oil consumption. *Most important of all, since the concession-*

*holder was now the British Admiralty, it no longer
had the patience to deal with internal riots, bartering with tribal khans, the Majlis [Parliament], and
the press.* It just wanted to deal with one person.
This is what led to the coup d'etat of 1299
A.H. (1919 A.D.), followed by the suppression of the
Kurds,[19] the defeat of Simitqu,[20] and the elimination
of Sheikh Khazal,[21] who could have founded an emirate
like Bahrain in Khuzestan if he had been a bit
smarter.

In our year 1311 (1932), the term of the D'Arcy
oil concession was about to expire. It was inevitable that the *principal owner of the concession--
the British Admiralty, i.e., the British government --*
would have to use such centralized power as there
was, with all its talk about a Majlis and ministries
to enable one person to control the army and public
security, to renew the concession while the iron was
hot. [Hassan] Taqi-Zadeh[22] became the 'instrument
for action'. A puppet assembly first voted to cancel
D'Arcy's concession, and then they renewed it with so
much propaganda that even the nation's elders didn't
guess the implications of that renewal, *or if they
knew they didn't say anything.* Why was there not a
whimper from any of them after this episode to ab-
solve them of history's condemnation? It was only
afterwards, when things began to fall apart for us,
that they began to try to head them off, years after
Shahrivar 1320 [September of 1941].[23]

Of course, such an ugly reality had to be
dressed up to suit the mood of the day. They compelled all the people to dress alike, took the men's
felt hats away from them, unveiled the women *as the
latest thing in progressive developments(!),* and
built a network of railroads--*not with oil money but
with taxes on sugar cubes and sugar*--whose primary
purpose happened to be to help provide access to the
Stalingrad front during World War II.

In 1320 (1941) there was war again in Europe,
the threat of Rashid 'Ali Gilani,[24] and a courtship
between the government of the day in Iran and the
Rome-Berlin axis as an *indication of maturity, but in
old age.* After all, *cows living in the same stable
will smell the same even if they can't get along with
each other.* It's no laughing matter, of course, and
we all saw what happened. All those high and mighty
powers, army, military police, military secret
police, and municipal police disintegrated in one

day. If Napoleon, the French commander in chief, was
satisfied to be sent to St. Helens, it was only
reasonable that the Iranian commander in chief would
put up with Mauritius Island.[¹⁵] Then it was the
United States of America which was looking ahead long
before World War II, and wanting the capability of
refueling its warships in the Persian Gulf. If you'd
been in their place, would you have been willing to
pay out dollars to refuel ships circling the world to
fight fascism--*that is, to save Russia and England?*
To an English oil company yet? Yes, United States
interference in Iranian politics started here, particularly in the Azarbaijan affair, where it was only
United States pressure that prompted the United Nations to act *and the Soviet Union to evacuate Azarbaijan.* Once again it was instability, liberation,
and talk of concessions for northern oil, held up as
a scarecrow by the British, who were unwilling to
surrender their harvest to the Americans.[¹⁶] There
was a brief period of freedom until 1329 (1951), when
oil was nationalized, America called 'check', and the
pawns were changed one after the other. One was
taken off the board and another was mated until
American capitalists were able to take over forty
percent of the stock in the oil consortium, the exact
amount that had been controlled by the British Admiralty. *And this is the story of the national
uprising of 28 Mordad 1332* [August 19, 1953].

This is what I call tagging along, /socially,/
politically, and economically, tagging along behind
the West, behind the oil companies, and behind
Western governments. This was the ultimate manifestation of <u>Gharbzadegi</u> in our time. This is how
Western industry controlled us, plundered us, and
managed our fate. It's obvious that when you've
turned over your country's economic and political op-
tions to foreign corporations, they know what to sell
to you and, at the very least, they know what not to
sell to you. Of course, for the one who wishes to
continue selling his manufactured goods, it's better
that you never get over your need for him. *And God
preserve the oil wells. They take the oil and give
you anything you want in return, from chicken milk to
human souls, even wheat.* This compulsory commerce
even goes on in our educational system, even in
literature and speech. Flip through the handful of
so-called substantive literary publications. What
information do they contain about this part of the
world? Or of the East generally? Of India, Japan,
or China? It all has to do with the Nobel Prize, *the*

changing of the pope, Francoise Sagan, the Cannes [Film Festival] prizes, or the latest Broadway play or Hollywood film. Popular photo magazines are even worse. *If we don't call them Weststruck then what is Weststruck?*

NOTES

[1]The fifth century legend of seven Christian soldiers who miraculously slept some three-hundred years in a cave near Ephesus. The story appears as a parable (The Companions of the Cave) in the Holy Qur'an, Surah XVIII, v. 9-26. (tr)

[2]The list of their names is very long, from Pietro della Valle to Eugene Flanden and Comte de Gobineau at the time of Nasr od-Din Shah. Fortunately, most of their writings have been translated. The best source of all for these expressions of delight is Zendegani-ye Shah Abbas [The life of Shah Abbas] by Nasr Allah Falsafi, recently published in three volumes. (A) [Translators' note: See Joseph Arthur Gobineau, Compte de, 1816-1882, Trois ans en Asie (de 1855 a 1858), (Paris: 1923), Eugene Napoleon Flanden, 1809-76, Voyage en Perse, (Paris: 1851-54), and Pietro della Valle, 1586-1652, Voyages dans la Turquie, l'Egypte, la Palestine, la Perse, les Indes Orientales et autres lieux, 3 vols. (Rouen: 1745). The Falsafi biography of Shah Abbas is now 5 volumes.]

[3]Sultan Husayn Bayqara, Timurid dynasty, who reigned from 1468 to 1506. (tr)

[4]A reference to the practice of granting trade concessions to Europeans followed by the Qajar shahs in nineteenth century Iran. (tr)

[5]The Ghilzais, a tribal group from Kandahar, revolted against the Safavid Shah Sultan Husayn I (1694-1722), and on March 8, 1722, routed the shah's forces and attained independence in the battle of Gulnabad. The Afghans effectively ended the Safavid dynasty later the same year by taking Isfahan. (tr)

[6]Shaykh Fazollah Nuri. See Richard W. Cottam, Nationalism in Iran (Pittsburgh: 1979), pp. 142-45, for more on Shaykh Nuri's activities and demise. (tr)

[7]This idea is taken from Sharh-e Hal-e Shahid Shaykh Nuri [Biography of the martyred Shaykh Nuri], by Dr. Tandar Kiya in the introduction of the most

recent Shahin (Tehran: 1335/1955), pp. 210-319. (A)

⁹A fatva is a legal ruling, or an expression of
opinion by one of the 'Ulama on a point of religious
law or a legal case. (tr)

⁹Brief biographies are to be found of Mirza
Malkum Khan and 'Abdul-Rahim Talibuff in H. Kamshad,
Modern Persian Prose Literature (New York/London/
Cambridge: 1966), pp. 14-16. (tr)

¹⁰See Taskhir-e Tamadun-e Farangi [The subjugation of European culture], by Sayyed Fakhr od-Din
Shadman, 1326/1947, which was undertaken before these
pages were written in search of a cure for the acute
pain of 'dandyism', and which proposed serious training in the mother tongue and the translation of
Arabic philosophical, literary, and scientific works.
Although he understood the sickness very well, he
didn't have a reliable prescription, because from
1326/1947 until today, although thousands of European
books have been translated, and we've all got a head
full of European knowledge, day by day we lean more
towards 'dandyism', and because this 'dandyism', or
as I like to put it, effeminacy, itself is one of the
simple symptoms of a deeper ailment, which is
'Gharbzadegi'. Dr. Mohammad Baqer may have gotten
closer to the root of this problem than anyone else.
Although reputed to be a Bahai, he wrote this in 1327
[21 Mar 1948-20 Mar 1949]: "You have looked through
the keyhole and seen that the Europeans are all
literate, but you haven't seen the stability in their
traditions and customs and you don't know that their
institutions of learning from kindergarten to the
university are all built on a church foundation, but
you've been destroying this foundation in your own
country for some time with Western earth-bound intellectualism, like someone serving cold soup in a hot
bowl!" (A)

¹¹In the treatises 'Islam, Akhund, va Hatef al-
Ghaib' [Islam, the clergy, and the voice of the un-
seen], 'Haftad ow Dow Millat' [Seventy-two nations],
'Resaleh-ye Yak Kalemeh' [One-word treatise],
'Siyasat-e Talebi' [The politics of Talebi], 'Siyahat
Nameh-ye Ebrahim Bek' [The itinerary of Ebrahim Bek],
etc... Most of these works are propaganda for
Gharbzadegi, and they amount to superstition posing
as religion. It is my belief that these things paved
the way for Gharbzadegi. (A)

[12]These are the words of Malkum Khan the Christian.   See   Majmu'eh-ye Asar-e Malkum Khan [The collected works of Malkum Khan], published by Mohit-e Tabataba'i (Tehran: 1328), and also Fekr-e Azad [Free thought], by Fereydoun Adamiyat (Tehran: 1340/1951), which very cleverly indicts one group of Freemasons and exonerates another, although Freemasons are all alike in my opinion. (A) [Translators' note: See also Hamid Algar, Mirza Malkum Khan: A Study in the History of Iranian Modernism (Berkeley: 1973), for more about this man's activities and those of other early Iranian proponents of Westernization.]

[13]The earlier edition used the Persian word for 'defect' ('eyb) instead of 'reason'('elat) here. (tr)

[14]Mirza Hassan Shirazi--see Nikkie R. Keddie, Religion and Rebellion in Iran: The Tobacco Protest of 1891-92 (London: 1966). (tr)

[15]A dilemma arises for a Muslim performing daily prayers if he or she happens to forget which prostration in the prescribed sequence comes next, since it is forbidden to break the ritual and begin anew. In Iran a considerable amount of clerical attention has been devoted to determining the proper steps to take in such cases, and this is what the author is belittling here. (tr)

[16]In the interval between the first and second printings of this booklet a book was published called Marja'iyyat va Rowhaniyyat [Marja'iyyat and the clergy], Dey 1341 [22 Dec-20 Jan 1963], (Tehran: Sherkat-e Enteshar) full of clerical language, but calling for relative intelligence and awareness concerning these issues and responsibilities, and with solutions, especially in the articles by Engineer [Mehdi] Bazargan, a university professor, and Sayyed Mahmud Taleqani, Emam of the Hedayat Mosque. They suggested a kind of council for issuing fatvas instead of one marja'-e taqlid [model for imitation]. If we agree that this booklet, with all its defects, was prophetic in a way of the events of 15 Khordad 1342 [June 5, 1963], now that a year has passed since those events I will be presumptuous and address these remarks to the clerical officials. If the clergy is going to:

A - Ignore its own principles, one of which I mentioned, and

*B - Continue to amuse itself with trivia and
pronouncing this and that to be un-Islamic and un-
believing and*
  *C - Forget that by relying on the principle of
ejtehad and the fatva the way is more open for the
Shi'is than the Sunnis for accepting the changes of
time (when the fatva on women's freedom was given by
Shaykh Mahmud Shaltut, Regent of Al Azhar University
and not the Shi'i clergy), in any case if the clergy
can't break open that cocoon of the dawn of the Constitutional Revolution, we have no choice but to accept the fact that this last bastion of defense
against Gharbzadegi has lost its vitality and spirit
and become a petrified fossil fit only for a museum,
or at best it has become the last refuge for all the
reactionary powers.* (A) [Translators' notes: On June
5, 1963, massive demonstrations took place in Tehran,
Shiraz, Varamin, Kashan, and Mashhad protesting
Ayatollah Khomeini's arrest. A recapitulation of
these events and their background, as well as a contemporary perspective on the Iranian clergy at the
time Al-e Ahmad wrote Gharbzadegi is in Hamid Algar,
"The Oppositional Role of the 'Ulama in Twentieth-
Century Iran," published in Scholars, Saints, and
Sufis, Muslim Religious Institutions Since 1500,
Nikkie R. Keddie, ed., (Berkeley, Los Angeles: 1972),
pp. 231-235. Taleqani and Bazargan, both of whom
were prominent figures in the Revolution of 1978-79,
were involved at the time Gharbzadegi was written in
a movement to modernize Shi'i Islam. The movement's
concerns and issues are discussed in detail in Nikkie
R. Keddie, "A Reconsideration of the Position of Marja'-e Taqlid and the Religious Institution," Studia
Islamica 20 (1964): 115-135. Ejtehad is the competence to exercise independent judgment on matters
related to religious law. In Iran this capability is
generally thought to be possessed only by the clergy.
The Emam of a mosque is its congregational prayer
leader. Marja'-e taqlid is the title of a Shi'i
clergyman with a following that has voluntarily
chosen to accept the religious obligation of adhering
to his judgments on matters of religious law. Marja'iyyat is the name for the authority exercised by
such a clergyman.]

  [17]William Knox D'Arcy--see Cottam, op. cit., p
200. (tr)

  [18]*You'll remember that one of the British
Petroleum stockholders was Commander As'ad
Bakhtiyari, like Moshir od-Dowleh (Nasrollah Khan).*

If they had destroyed this commander As'ad during
Reza Shah's time don't you think that he also, like
Shaykh Khaz'al, who had land claims in Khuzestan,
would have had land claims in the Bakhtiyari tribe's
Winter quarters and been a problem for the government
of the time? And again just like the Hayat Davudis,
who had claims on Khark Island and were shot as a
result...? For more on these matters see *Tala-ye
Siyah ya Bala-ye Iran* [Black gold or disaster for
Iran] by Abol Fazl Lesani. (A)

[19]See Cottam, op. cit., pp. 67-68. (tr)

[20]Aqa Isma'il Simitqu--see ibid., p. 70. (tr)

[21]Known also as the Sheikh of Mohammarah--see
ibid., pp. 111-14. (tr)

[22]Sayyed Hassan Taqi-Zadeh, liberal minority
leader of Tabriz. See Peter Avery, Modern Iran (New
York: 1967), pp. 270-71. (tr)

[23]The month of Shahrivar, 1320 A.H., when Reza
Shah abdicated in favor of his son, Mohammad Reza
Pahlavi (September 16, 1941). (tr)

[24]See Cottam, op. cit., pp. 72-73. (tr)

[25]Reza Shah went to Mauritius after abdicating.
(tr)

[26]See Cottam, op. cit., pp. 198-221. (tr)

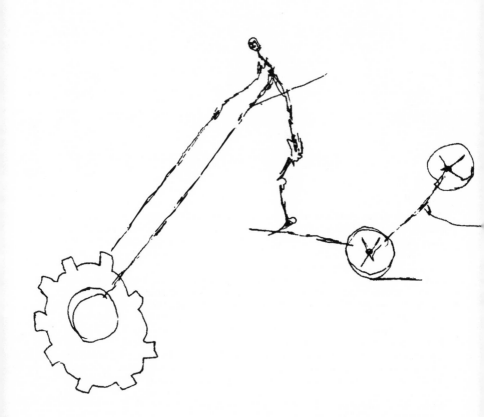

ARDESHIR·82

5

MISCELLANEOUS CONFLICTS

We now resemble a strange nation with an unknown tradition and a culture that neither has its roots in our land nor flourishes the way it did originally. In our daily life, in our politics, and in our culture, everything we have is inadequate. /I don't know anymore to whom the promise of Islam, "We have given thee abundance,"[1] was made. /And who is this 'thee', anyway? Something consisting of nineteen- to twenty-million human beings. Seventy-five percent of them live in villages, tents, *or huts* with customs from the dawn of creation, ignorant of new values, condemned to a master-servant lifestyle, unfamiliar with machines, with tools made for primitive tasks, and with food, fuel, clothing, and homes all belonging to a primitive life: *plows, barley bread, steer manure, canvas [clothing], and shacks.* The only Western influences that have reached these villages are military conscription and transistor radios. Both of them are more destructive than dynamite.

Powerful

Machines bring changes, and the first step is the replacement of [charcoal-burning] <u>korsis</u> with [oil-burning] space heaters, but in these villages of ours they don't even know about charcoal, let alone oil. /They use steer manure for fuel./

We, who are a petroleum-rich nation, and *expend*

73

a lot of effort promoting increased oil consumption at that, consume only 250 liters of gasoline and kerosene per person per year.[2] Furthermore, with all these four-wheeled wrecks we have in our cities *burning gasoline and running into each other,* and all this kerosene, most of us can't even cook a pot of eshkaneh[3] once a day. On top of that, our Gharbzadegi demands that we inundate these very villages with the various kinds of tractors we have to buy, directly proportionate to our oil exports, with credit from our oil sales. What do these tractors do? They plow under all our ancestral structures and boundaries!

And look at the murderous violence that erupts when one of these twentieth-century blind plows strays a few inches from Kal Madd Vali's land onto Kal 'Abbas 'Ali's land.[4] I've assembled an archive full of these bloody clashes, *and accounts of heads being split open with shovels, for a story.* Yet, in such circumstances, they've decided that dividing land among the peasants[5] is the last word in village transformation, and in extending the class of petty landowners! And extending the class of petty landowners means that all arable land must be converted to a huge spider web of individual plots that will snare every machine that comes by *and destroy its capacity to operate.*

Look what a graveyard our nation's farmlands have become for the corroding wrecks of these machines and tractors, which have no convenient repair facilities to maintain them, *where there's no open horizon or extensive mass of land where they can be put to good use, and no road to take them to the city for repairs.* With all this, the villagers are completely idle at least three months out of the year! They're plagued by cold weather, freezing, dryness, drought, and locusts. *When are we going to solve these problems, anyway?*

If the food in an advanced, industrialized country is produced by nine to fifteen percent of the population, we delegate sixty percent of the people in this country to the task of providing for our stomachs. In spite of this, every year we import wheat from the United States and sugar from Formosa. We who are supposedly living in an agricultural country! And what do those zealous villagers do during the nine months out of the year when they work? They chop grass, *dry manure in the sun, drive*

their sheep to the water's edge, observe the ritual
prayers, or pray for rain. "This isn't work, after
all! The transistor radios say people in the cities
are making money by the shovelful. *Every Wednesday.*'
So let's go!" They leave the villages group by
group, headed for the cities, where able-bodied young
men have already been taken to join the army, work as
domestic servants, or engage in busywork or idleness.
They go to the cities where the remaining twenty-five
percent of the zealous population is protected from
the ravages of time under mud roofs behind high,
thick walls. /To the cities where able-bodied young
men march about in ranks on the army posts and in the
streets./ To cities that are mostly overblown villages or, in the words of my friend Hoseyn Malek,
just tangles straddling the secondary roadways.

Mone
romanticism

     These cities are just flea markets hawking
European manufactured goods. In Yazd alone one can
see fifty years' worth of the Raleigh bicycle factory's production. A month's worth of the Mitsubishi
factory's output is in Torbat-e Heydariyeh, and there
are ten years' worth of Fords, Chevrolets, and Fiats
in Tehran. And then you can't buy butter in Kerman
and you have to eat Australian canned goods in
Tabriz. *I've had all these experiences.* Yes. We
flee those villages to these cities. To the crowded
city jungles. To do what? *To watch automobiles for
tips and sell lottery tickets*, or if we're really
capable we get to mix mud and straw. What's the pay?
Lunch, and if there's a market for construction,
seven *to ten* tumans [$1-$1.45] a day, *which is the
hourly wage of a common laborer in the industrial
countries.*

     It's true that this sort of urbanization is in-
exorably expanding. In what age, however, have you
ever heard of a city that could survive without villages? The way we are, in no time at all instead of
cities and villages we'll have heaps of dilapidated
machines all over the country, all of them exactly
like American junkyards, and as big as Tehran. /Yes,
this is how we are becoming urbanized./ These
machines, after all, unlike a mountain cannon, can't
be mounted on mule-back and transported with a
migrating tribe from this mountain to that hill for
protection and security.

     Even if you buy a Peugeot, you have to hustle to
find a shelter for it at night, because if you don't
the cold will crack the radiator, and then how will

you keep up the payments? This is why we have a lot
of cab drivers in our cities who sleep in dingy
flophouses for two tumans [thirty cents] a night with
their taxis parked in a parking lot that costs one
tuman [fifteen cents] a night. And in this climate
of ours at that!

Yes. The constraints of machine consumption /and
technology/ are bringing urbanization, and this urbanization is the sequel to being uprooted from the
land.

In order to migrate to the city you must flee
your father's land, or flee a feudal village, or grow
weary of the roaming of tribal life *and escape.* This
is the first conflict that has produced our
Gharbzadegi. In order to respond to the machine's
call for urbanization, you uproot the people lock,
stock, and barrel from the villages and send them to
the cities, which have neither work nor shelter for
newcomers, while the machines themselves, meanwhile,
have also worked their way into the villages. *And
even though a machine does the work of ten men and
their overseers, even in the village a machine is not
without the need for service. And technical service.
And where do you get this? You can see how terribly
chaotic things have become!*

We have other conflicts arising out of this same
Gharbzadegi. Let's enumerate them.

The first priorities of urban life are food for
the stomach and sex for what's below the stomach, and
in order to obtain these things, we concern ourselves
with attire (appearances),' because we couldn't get
these things in the village. The enterprises of the
new bourgeoisie, therefore, are food industries,
(sugarcube-making, *cookies, vegetable oil, compote,
and pasteurized milk,*) construction industries (concrete mixing, *fancy brick-making, mosaics, and so
on...*), and garment industries (*textiles, tricot,
General Mode,*' *and so on...*). Moreover, with our
centuries-old chronic poverty and poor nutrition,
this in itself was a step forward. Such a chronically starved individual, *who's eaten bread and dugh'
all his life in the village,* once he's filled his
stomach *with a sandwich in the city,* will go to the
barber and the tailor, then for a shoeshine, and then
to a whorehouse.

Political parties and organizations are forbidden. *I don't know what to say about your clubs and this sort of thing.* Mosques and altars have been forgotten, *and if they aren't forgotten, they are only attended during the months of Moharram and Ramazan.* In place of all these things there are cinemas,[10] television, and publications that imprint the mannerisms and dress of movie stars on thousands of eager urbanites every day. Where will they get food for all these people? From the villages. Villages that have been emptied, with all the cattle slaughtered, the ganats [underground canals][11] dried up, where the #5 screw for the deep-well pump has been broken, tractor plows are rusted and corroded, and even if the company orders them it takes at least a year to get spare parts. After all, an entire city cannot be fed on donated American powdered milk or Australian wheat!

Another conflict. Urban life requires security, whether in a city or in a village. We saw, furthermore, that the villages are being emptied out and that most of them and many of our cities are still in the path of tribal migrations, migrations that trample *and devour* the crops, destroy the creeks, throw dead dogs into the ganats, steal chickens, and bring insecurity. As a result, we don't even have security in our small cities, let alone in the villages. For this reason, the people of this country don't trust each other. Two-faced and conditioned to using the principle of taqiyeh [dissimulation][11], they hide from the evil of the calamities of the day behind high adobe or cement walls.

If the high walls around the cities once reduced the need for a wall around every house, today, when we've destroyed the walls *and gates* encircling the cities to make way for streets--passageways for bulldozers, tractors, *trucks*, /and automobiles/--we must have a wall around every house. And such high walls! Our land is a land of salt deserts and high walls. Clay walls in the villages and brick *and concrete* walls in the cities. This is not confined to the external world. Similar walls have been built up to the sky around every person's inner world as well. Everyone is withdrawn behind an individual wall of pessimism, superstition, mistrust, and individualism.

On the other hand, I mentioned that the villager or town-dweller living in a community has either fled his masters in the village or his tribe, or he has gotten himself out of the way of the annual tribal

migration, which brings an invasion and sneaky
plundering along with it, in order to find a secure
place for himself in the city or in such-and-such a
community. But what they don't realize is that when
the same tribal chief gets into the government ten
years later and sets up such-and-such a dynasty
(*tribal rather than royal*), he'll either turn over
the very same city in which they [the villagers or
town-dwellers] have taken refuge to some khan's feifdom, or else he'll give the feifdom some village with
its newly dug ganat, and they'll be right back where
they started. The last partitioning of feifdoms we
had was during the Constitutional Revolution, and
with this brand of feudalism[13] *and tribal migration
that we still have*, God knows how long we'll be suf-
fering from the side effects of control by khans,
migration, insecurity, uncertainty, pessimism, *and
despair of tomorrow*. In what age is all this taking
place? In an era when machines themselves are not
only the most powerful feudal lord of all, sitting in
the seat of the Lord of lords, but when they are also
demanding security, open borders, no walls,
simplicity, *or better yet, credulity*, faith in the
other person, *and faith in tomorrow*.

There is another conflict. When the machines
arrived and became established in the cities and
villages--whether they were motorized mills or textile factories--they put the workers in the local industries out of work. They retired the village mill.
They rendered the spinning wheel useless, and retired
the carpet weavers and felt makers. Because of these
local handicrafts--because of carpets, tiles, hand-
printed textiles, and giveh [cloth shoes][14]--our
markets thrived to some extent. We're at a loss now
to explain why our markets are inactive or our carpet
trade in foreign markets is endangered, and we're
unprepared to deal with the fact that this is only
the beginning, and that when machines get a foothold
in the villages and become widespread, we are in for
more disruptions. I have personally observed that
all the windmills between Qa'in and Gunabad are inactive, like slain demons out of legends or old village
and hamlet guards gone to sleep. In Dizful alone,
with its beautiful brickwork and classic city design,
I saw almost one-hundred inactive windmills. When
machines get a foothold in the villages they'll
destroy all supplementary pastoral and village
economic activity, meaning all local industries and
handicrafts. And what could be better, than that all
these young people's eyes, chests, and hands not be

ruined in front of a carpet loom just to beautify the
homes of the aristocracy /(may it perish)/? The
saving grace of the mechanization of agriculture and
village life is *not merely* that it will disrupt
master-servant relationships and destroy the practices of migration, nomadic life, and feudalism, *but
there is also the fact that the regional industries
and handicrafts will either disappear, or, if there's
a plan with a program to preserve them, it can give
them more money and prestige, because in the event of
the existence of preservation programs it would be
possible to raise salaries because new buyers for
handicrafts could be found, because the market for
cloth shoes could be expanded, and so on....*

Another conflict. The implements of primitive
life, from plowshares, <u>korsis</u>, <u>givehs</u>, and kerosene
lamps to sickles, spinning wheels, and carpet looms,
bring primitive thinking along with them or vice versa. Belief in superstition--banging washtubs during
eclipses of the sun and moon, certain kinds of
prayer, talismans, conjuring to avoid sickness and
misfortune, *advice from Kolsum Naneh, the fortune-
teller*--all are examples of this kind of thinking.[15]
*Of course this kind of thinking has to go when
machines come, but don't think it will happen this
fast.* These same superstitious *and fortune-telling*
people are the ones who *now* swarm into the cities and
become the slaves of machines, or become bulldozer
and tractor operators in their own villages. People
don't just materialize out of thin air, *and we don't
import them along with the machines. At least one
school cycle will be required to give these people
modern--machine--training.* I saw a <u>nazar-e qorbani</u>[16]
hanging from the steering wheel of a bulldozer
operator's huge machine as he was clearing Khark Island! Our taxis are full of these same magic charms,
our shops full of prayers, curses, and verses that
say "Let it be," or "Live for today."

It is under these conditions that a man will
suddenly become a gangster and rob a bank. The
primitive man who comes to the city and girds himself
for machine service must keep pace with machines,
even with all his mental dullness, his physical laziness, and all his beliefs in predestination, and he
must react at the same pace as them. This man, who
believes in predestination, tells fortunes by opening
books at random or consulting a rosary, makes holiday
sacrifices, and accepts soup offered as devotional
charity as his due, is now involved with machines,

which have no notion of the fate of a thing. His
brakes will engage no more quickly nor will his motor
run more slowly because of his monthly sacrifices.
*So, when his monthly sacrifice has no effect and he
keeps having accidents, he suddenly gets fed up,
knuckles under, and either turns out completely
apathetic and a criminal or just drifts with the
wind.*

         Another conflict. One of the responsibilities
of <u>Gharbzadegi,</u> or one of its requirements, is granting freedom to women. Apparently we had a need for
this fifty percent of our nation's power, so we ordered society to make way for the arrival of the
women's caravan! But how have we done this? Are
women and men equal in all respects? We've been
satisfied to forcibly remove their veils, with much
fanfare, and to open some of the schools for them.
Beyond that, nothing. That's enough for them.

         Women are incapable of judging. They cannot
serve as witnesses.[17] Voting and serving as a representative in the Majlis [Parliament] has been a joke
for a long time.[18] Even men have no real rights in
this, and there are no real elections. Divorce is
the man's prerogative, and how well we have used and
expounded on the phrase, "Men are in charge of
women"![19] What have we really done? We have simply
given women permission to display themselves in
society. Just a display. *That is, exhibitionism.*
We have placed women, who are the protectors of
tradition, the family, bloodlines, and the generations, in a position of irresponsibility. We've
brought them into the streets, to exhibit themselves,
to be without duties, to make up their faces, to wear
new styles every day and to hang around. But come
now, work, duties, responsibility, either personal or
social? Never! *That is, women of this sort are
still very few. As long as the value of the social
services of men and women and the value of their work
(their salaries) are unequal, and as long as the
woman doesn't take on the responsibility of managing
some corner of society (other than the home, which is
an internal and shared matter between husband and
wife) shoulder to shoulder with the man, and as long
as there is no material and spiritual equality between these two, there will be no point in this
feigned liberation of women for years and years to
come* except to create additions to the pool of consumers who use face powder and rouge produced by
Western industry. This is the other side of

Gharbzadegi. Of course, we're talking about the
cities. We're talking about our national leadership,
which is inaccessible to women, while in the tribes
and villages, for centuries women have carried the
primary burden of life on their shoulders.[20]

There is another conflict that is very complicated *and no one even notices it*: Ninety percent of
the people in this country live by religious values
and criteria. *I'm talking about that ninety percent
of all the villagers, in addition to the urban merchant and bazaari classes, menial service workers,
and all of what makes up the country's third and
fourth classes. These classes, in their poverty, can
only tolerate this /dog's/ life of theirs by falling
back on religious beliefs. Inevitably they look for
today's unrealized happiness in the sky, in religion,
and in the hereafter.* /At least they have the good
fortune to be believers, in a religion, in a sky, in
another world, in good and evil,/ and so much the
better for them! They even drink alchoholic
beverages sometimes, but then they cleanse their
mouths with water and stand to prayer. They perform
their prayers and repent during the month of
Ramazan,[21] and they even make sacrifices to Emamzadeh
Davud,[22] /to say nothing of God/, at the Kaaba[23] or
during the Feast of Sacrifice.[24] Our villager, as
soon as he gets a ten-seed return on the seven seeds
he planted, will take his wife and children by the
hand and make a pilgrimage to Mashhad, or at least to
Qom, and if our relations with our neighbors are good
he will go to Karbala--and Mecca *if he can*. And
everyone is waiting for the Imam of the Age. I mean
all of us are waiting, and rightfully so, because no
secular government has come through on the least of
its promises, and because oppression is everywhere,
rights are everywhere usurped, and there is suffoca-
tion and discrimination!

It is for all these reasons that our huge
celebration of the fifteenth of Sha'ban[25] puts Nowruz
[the Iranian New Year] to shame. These beliefs lead
ninety percent of the population to consider the
(secular) government *an oppressor and* the usurper of
the rightful place of the Imam of the Age (His Holiness the Crown Prince of the Age, may God hasten His
joyful advent). Therefore they're justified in not
paying their taxes, duping government agents, avoid-
ing conscription on a thousand pretexts, and never
giving accurate information to the census takers.
Even if the newspapers are full of stories about how

[handwritten margin notes:] I agree with this. Gov' can't solve all ar problems

the people of Mazlaqan Chay have welcomed the person-
nel in the newly installed government Bureau of Vital
Statistics, in reality, the zealous inhabitants of
that village are not the least bit aware of any
government organization, save the gendarmes and the
transistor radios.

A proverb is still current in Bushahr and Bandar
Abbas that goes "It is unwise to take a nap in the
shade of an 'ajam's'' wall."'' This 'ajam is the
government, and the idea is that one should not become a slave to the government, nor put one's faith
in its *agents and* institutions. Under such circumstances, all the religious establishments, from
the drinking barrel under the awning and the mosque
down the street to the shrine outside the village,
are full of different demonstrations of nonconfidence
in the government and its activities. They are
covered with various signs anticipating the relief
the promised Mahdi, His Holiness the Crown Prince of
the Age, will bring (May God hasten His joyful advent!), expressed in the language of the people, in
the calligraphy at the tops of the walls, in the language of the preachers, in our prayers, in the call
to prayers, in litanies, in the poetry of the poets,
in the elaborate demonstrations on the fifteenth of
Sha'ban and at the tops of wedding invitations....
*Every place lives "in the shadow of expectation of
the Crown Prince."* All this is true!

Meanwhile, *it is for these people that* the
government, with its organizations, schools, military
installations, administrative offices, *prisons, and
the trumpets and horns of its radios,* promotes
nationalism, plays a different tune of its own,
pleads for taxes from these same people, conscripts
soldiers from them by force, fosters corruption
everywhere, and has the most degenerate embassies in
the world, *missionaries for the other 'His Excellency'.* The fanfare and propaganda of its radio stations have deafened the ears of heaven with *thousands
and thousands of never-ending* claims to glory; it
continually points its cannons and rifles into the
people's faces and /has its twenty-five-hundred-year
exhibition in Shiraz and stages a seven-thousand-year
exposition in Paris/!

Because of this conflict, every elementary
school child forgets his prayers when he memorizes
the Imperial Anthem as his national anthem. By the
time he reaches the sixth grade he's stopped going to

the mosque. He relegates his religion to oblivion the first time he goes to a movie. This is why ninety percent of our high school graduates are ag- nostics. No, they aren't even agnostics. They just don't think about these things at all. They're in a vacuum. They have no firm footing anywhere. No cer- tainty, no faith. This is because they see that the government, with all its puffing and blowing, its or- ganization, its budget, its foreign aid, cannot solve the slightest social problem, *which might be unemployment among high school graduates*. And at the same time you can see what a wonderful refuge an an- cient belief is for swarms of distressed and poverty- stricken people. *And how they rejoice, and how happy they are on the fifteenth of Sha'ban*. This is what disturbs them. The radio has them under its spell constantly, the cinema brings them visions of more sophisticated lifestyles, while that other reality is still there, unnoticed, *a reality of religious faith*. But how much can one think, contain one's anger, or seek to discover the truth? Why not just give that up too, /say "whatever will be will be",/ and be like everyone else *and blend in with society?* Let's just all float with the tide, *with no sign of our religion, nor any sign of our irreligion, no sign of our life, nor of our future,* saying *"Live for today"*.[21]

Everyone in the Ministry of Education knows that our schools are training white-collar workers--or unemployed high school graduates. There's no disput- ing that. What's even clearer *and remains unsaid* is that our schools are fostering <u>Gharbzadegi</u>. They're turning out failures, *people prepared to accept* <u>Gharbzadegi</u>. This is the greatest danger in our schools and our educational system. I'll give a full description of this person who comes out of our westernizing factories in another chapter.

What I must say now is that, contrary to the opinion of our bearded and mustachioed historians, our Shu'ubi[22] political and religious movements have never gotten us anywhere--*I'm talking about the move- ments that carry their rhetoric on nationalism and religion to extremes*. And if they did, the founda- tions they laid were built up to a completed edifice in the time of the Safavids, because at that time the church and the state--*the authorities and the clergy*--put on the same robe, and both of their hands came out the same sleeve. *In the first parts of the booklet I explained what these strange bedfellows produced together, historically and generally. And confidentially, you will remember that we also had such a situation in the Sassanid period, which resulted in the Mani and Mazdak uprisings, and ultimately in the emergence of Islam.* But today, when that common robe has been torn to shreds and church and state each have their own separate organizations, customs, and regulations, things are even worse for us *than they were during those two periods.* As disunity has come between the religious establishment and the present government, things have deteriorated to the point that our government, leaning towards <u>Gharbzadegi</u> and encouraging the imitation of foreigners, leads the country day by day *down a road that will only end in ruin, decadence, and bankruptcy.*

The religious establishment, on the other hand, *with all its institutions and customs,* leans on superstition as much as it can. It seeks refuge in times long past and old outdated ceremonies, is satisfied to be the gatekeeper at the graveyard, and *in the twentieth century* thinks according to the criteria of the Middle Ages. These days, as the secular government hangs on to the coat tails of Europe and the West in an effort to stabilize itself, the *domestic* religious /shadow/ government stands in the ranks of the opposition, and regresses more and more as it tries to hold its ground.[10]

When the government and the ruling class see that ninety percent of the people pay no attention to their bewitchery, that they joyously congratulate each other on the birth of His Holiness the Crown Prince of the Age [Mahdi], when the state sees that the people have appropriated its official titles for their own purposes, that they don't accept the government, and when it sees the ground giving way beneath its feet, it has no choice but to cling ever more tightly to the coat tails of the West, to the coat tails of Europe-affectedness, and to rely on their military aid--*on donated American artillery and tanks, on the Western press,* on their products, their newspapers, their journalists, and their politicians--just to hang on for a few more days. Our government is such that it secretly oppresses the religious shadow government,[11] while promoting a national government. In order to confuse the people, the state announces the reclamation of Bahrein,[12] while contention over the Helmand and Shatt al-Arab rivers remains unresolved after two-hundred years. When is this happening? At a time when machines are

demanding open borders and deregulation, the removal
of all barriers to the internationalization of all
places, and common markets and duty-free importation.
With a United Nations flag in hand, they go
everywhere they can with their machines as long as
the *companies'* gasoline lasts.

Yet in this age we've withdrawn into our nation-
state *again*. Our common borders with our neighbors
are longer, thicker, /and more impenetrable/ than the
Great Wall of China. We're perpetually cut off from
the Iraqis, Afghanis, Pakistanis, and Russians.
We're in complete ignorance of one another, while in
the heart of Katanga a huge diamond-exporting cor-
porate organization shoots Dag Hammarskjold out of
the sky. In these times--with these schools, this
national anthem, this security organization [SAVAK],
this military aid, *this twenty-five-hundred-year
celebration*, with these cardboard people--we want to
promote our nation-state!

These days, frontiers everywhere in the world
are drawn solely along lines that define the domains
of various companies. One such line stakes out the
domain of General Motors, one that of Socony-Vacuum,
one that of Shell and British Petroleum, and one the
territory of Pan American or A.G.I.P. [Direzion] Mineraria.

These days, nations, languages, and races are
the playthings of orientalists(!), of whom I shall
have more to say later. *They're at least the subjects of laboratory experimentation for scientists,
scholars, and researchers.*[33] *And because of these
things no one bullies anyone in the twentieth century.* If I'm cut off from my Afghani brother of the
same *religion, tongue, and race,* and if it's harder
to come and go between Iraq and India than it is to
penetrate an iron wall, it's because we're in the
domain of one company and Afghanistan is a vital area
for another one. Under the conditions of these
times, the more tightly a nation's borders are
sealed, *the more racial traditions proliferate, the
more serious is the shah's raw pride and howling, and
the more influential the religious rulings on what is
allowable and unallowable,* the darker the blackness
of that national dungeon. Otherwise, what system or
boundary do you know of that would be impervious to
Pepsi Cola or to the import and export of petroleum?
Which of them would be inaccessible to a Brigitte
Bardot film, to heroin *smugglers,* or to those suspi-

cious orientalists, the official brokers of
colonialism? *The best example of these staked-out
domains--that is the most naked and blatant-and-
subtle-at-the-same-time of them--must be sought today
in Africa. There was a time when France had control
of Cameroun, Chad, and the central Sahara in three
parts of Africa. And the English had another state
next to each of these states. Today, when France and
England have left and them would be inaccessible to a
Brige?tte Bardot film, function, each one has drawn
its borders exactly where the colonialist boundaries
of such-and-such a foreign government were--and what
a lot of African tribes, races, and religions have
been chopped up this way among Africa's contemporary
independent self-determinant governments...but let me
continue.*

Perhaps we all remember how they--*the nation's
elders*--used the religious establishment, meaning the
religious shadow government, to attain their objectives in the fight to nationalize petroleum. Confidentially, in those days the leaders of the people
had the intelligence to depict the struggle in such a
way that, *with the help of the religious leaders,*
every uneducated person would view the ruling class
as the instrument of oppression, which gave oil to
the companies and drew its sabres on the people.
*This is the biggest lesson the intellectuals and
leaders ought to have learned from those events.*[14]

As for the last conflict arising out of
__Gharbzadegi__, and the most dangerous of them all, I
must again say very confidentially that we're located
in a part of the world where great events are taking
place right under our noses, of which we are kept in
compulsory ignorance. These things are not permitted
to influence us, irrespective of whether we want them
to or not. *And if we do receive influences from
them, it's only in a superficial way for the purpose
of putting the matter aside.* Yet Cuba, 130
kilometers from the United States itself, receives
influences from these events and not a thing happens!
It may be because the walls surrounding us are so
thick already and our government pays no attention to
the hidden religious government (itself a wall inside
the other wall and a government within a government)
that day by day the thickness of this wall, with a
leaning toward __Gharbzadegi__ and an insistence on
obedience to the West, increases!

Maybe they imagine that, confronted with such

neighborhood danger, our only way out is to take refuge in the cocoon of prejudice, rigidity, ignorance, and medieval rancor, while *nowadays* the fate of /small/ states and the *flags and* borderlines of the world are decided among the big powers at the conference table. Our governments in this part of the world are satisfied to police borders for the companies. It is for this reason as well that our government, while suppressing religion and sheltering agnostics and Europophiles--since it has a need to dupe the people--usually displays an indifferent attitude towards religion and the spiritual community while carrying on a political charade with those in religious circles and their leaders.

In any case, all these things are merely the flopping and thrashing of a butchered animal. If, in close proximity to these great events, we don't make a move ourselves to stop these qualitative disputes in their tracks, even if the boundaries of the state become one-thousand times stronger, even if we thwart the religious establishment one-thousand times by deluding its leaders to prevent them from penetrating and weakening the foundation of that wall from within, ultimately, because of the very elementary law that water always seeks its own level, this swamp will rise and all our flimsy thatch castles will be inundated. *I'm not talking about threats and intimidation. I explained where the center of these threats and intimidation has been moved to at the beginning of the booklet. I'm talking about compatibility with the progressive societies of humanity.* Excuse me for not being more explicit.

NOTES

[1]The Holy Qur'an, Surah CVIII, v. 1. (tr)

[2]Total consumption of petroleum products in Iran (not including tar and medicines derived from petroleum) was 3,900,000 metric tons in 1960. Say four million. Divide by twenty million people and you get two-hundred liters per year. (A)

[3]Eshkaneh is an egg-drop soup made from water, eggs, onion, butter, salt, and turmeric. It is very inexpensive to make. The reference to it here adds further emphasis to the author's image of the deprived, fuel-poor condition of the common Iranian living in a land awash with oil. (tr)

[4]The two names are fictitious inventions. They suggest two characters who have known all their lives how to live together side-by-side according to a well-understood set of rules. But no rules come with the tractors. Kal is slang for Karbala'i, the title given to someone who has made a religious pilgrimage to Karbala, Iraq. (tr)

[5]A reference to the Shah's White Revolution. (tr)

[6]Wednesdays were the days the Bongah-e Bakht-e Azma'i [Lottery Foundation] held drawings and announced the week's winners, who were allowed to shovel money from a pile of small change for fifteen minutes. What was left was supposedly given to charitable causes. (tr)

[7]"Precise statistics show that Iran ranks sixteenth among the nations of the world in beauty parlors and barber shops... In Tehran there are 22,000 licensed barber shops and beauty parlors and 25,000 unlicensed ones in operation. By comparing this with London, which has 42,000 barber shops and beauty parlors, and Moscow which has 39,000, one can see the extent to which the people of Tehran have emphasized their physical appearance in the last few years." From Ferdowsi (weekly) magazine, Wednesday, 21 Khordad, 1342 [June 11, 1963], p. 2. (A)

*General Mode was the name of a large Tehran department store. (tr)

*Dugh is yogurt diluted with water. (tr)

[10]*"The cinema, along with narcotics and cigarettes, has become a haven for those seeking to escape their anxieties, their homes, their families, and for those fleeing the schools and sexual and. other deprivations. In Tehran alone people go to the cinema thirty-three million times a year and spend fifteen million rials [$215,000]." From Majalleh-ye Masa'el-e Iran Azar, 1342 [22 Nov-21 Dec 1963] from the article "Sinema va Mardom az Yakdegar Cheh Mikhwahand?" [What do the cinema and the people want from each other?]. The same article quoted several lines on this same cinema issue from Ketab-e Iran [Book on Iran] which is a report on Iran by sixteen American specialists (1958): "In the film, the Iranian who leans towards the West finds that new civilization which he has been promised in his new teaching and training and of which he or she is deprived in life. For him or her the cinema is an escape from a society full of disappointment, and a refuge in a utopian world in which his or her Western values are realized...." (A)

[11]*Qanats are subterranean passages connecting a village or a city to an alluvial fan for a permanent water supply. They commonly extend great distances and require years of work to construct. (tr)

[12]*Taqiyeh in Shi'i Islam is the theologically sanctioned practice of lying about one's intention or belief in order to avoid persecution. It was introduced when Sunni caliphs ruled the Islamic world and the Shi'is and their Imams faced a real threat of persecution. (tr)

[13]*"Until the mid-nineteenth century, Iran had a social system which might be termed 'tribal feudalism', although a phrase encompassing both tribal and upper-class urban dominance of the countryside would be better. Beginning in the eleventh century A.D., a large proportion of landholdings were under essentially feudal land grants, based on governmental, religious, or military service. The conduct of war was largely in the hands of tribal leaders, who held some of these grants, and feudal dues and services were demanded of the peasantry, the main productive class. Iranian

feudalism differed from Western feudalism in the following respects: the lack of feudal contracts and of
serfdom; the residence of Iranian ruling classes in
the cities rather than on manors; the prevalence of
nomadic tribes, leading to frequent wars and destructive raids; and the importance of water control and
irrigation." From Nikkie R. Keddie, Iran: Religion,
Politics, and Society, (London, Totowa, N.J.: Cass
Publications, 1980), p. 159. (tr)

    [14]See Hans E. Wulff, The Traditional Crafts of
Persia (Cambridge, Mass.: M.I.T. Press, 1966), for a
technical description of the manufacture of the giveh
(cloth shoe) in Iran and a discussion of the impact
of Western influence on this and other Iranian handicrafts. (tr)

    [15]My brother-in-law, Manuchehr Daneshvar, saw
people praying for rain during the New Year holidays
this year in Aqa Jari, one of the oil-exporting
centers! Each of the women was holding up a kid or a
sheep saying "Oh God, even if we are sinners unworthy
of mercy, what have these dumb animals done?" (A)

    [16]Here, a nazar-e qorbani is a windshield orna-
ment of some kind intended to ward off misfortune
caused by envious or 'evil' eyes. It is used in the
belief that envious glances from others cause bad
luck. Animal sacrifices, known by the same name, are
used to protect young children from the eyes of envious women. (tr)

    [17]The author is here referring to the status of
women in the courts according to Islamic law. He is
correct in that women have been effectively excluded
from serving as judges throughout Islamic history,
although there are exceptions to this. It is by no
means true that women are not allowed to testify in a
court as witnesses, although their rights in this are
limited, and they are forbidden to testify in certain
types of cases. These restrictions are based on
interpretations that have become established in Islamic jurisprudence derived from a Qur'anic verse
equating two women witnesses with a single male wit-
ness, and a sometimes-disputed tradition in which the
prophet Mohammad states that women are deficient in
reason. We cannot do justice to the Islamic view of
sexual specialization in a footnote, but we caution
non-Muslim readers who have yet to consider this
facet of Islamic civilization not to form opinions--
especially opinions based on Al-e Ahmad's remark as

translated here--without first getting the views of Muslim women on the subject. Many of them find that their place in society as defined by Islamic tradition is not only acceptable, but much to be preferred over the politically equal, but unprotected, status of Western women. (tr)

¹⁸The Iranian Majlis of 1962 was a strictly secular body with very little resemblance to the Majlis that was formed after the revolution under Khomeini. The religious restrictions on the rights of women listed here were not officially the law of the land at that time. Theoretically at least, their observance or nonobservance was optional and a matter of religious belief. Yet even in 1962 a large part of the population considered Islamic law binding in their lives. (tr)

¹⁹The Holy Qur'an, Surah IV, v. 34. This verse has also been translated, "Men are the protectors and maintainers of women." (tr)

²⁰In the interval between the first and second printings of this booklet certain things have happened in these provinces, among them the in-name-only liberation of the ladies. There are even women taking part in the puppet shows in the Senate and the Majlis. But this liberation of women makes about as much sense as plastering over the walls and doors of a royal tomb. All without substance, empty talk, empty gestures, and for the purpose of faking foreign policy at that. Yet with all that don't you think a dam has been broken? (A)

²¹Ramazan is the ninth month of the Islamic lunar calendar. It is incumbent upon all Muslims to observe a daylight fast during this time. (tr)

²²The tomb and shrine of a descendant of one of the Twelve Imams. (tr)

²³The most important shrine in Islam, called the Kaaba or House of God (Bayt Allah), located almost in the center of the Grand Mosque in Mecca. Muslims throughout the world direct their prayers in its direction, and it is the goal of the Hajj, or pilgrimage to Mecca. (tr)

²⁴This day is set aside in Muslim ritual on the tenth day of the month of Dhu al-Hijja in the Islamic lunar calendar for sacrificial offerings to God. The

term (<u>'Eyd-e Qorban</u>) also refers to a four-day feast taking place on this and the following three days, the last four days of the calendar period set aside for the <u>Hajj</u>. (tr)

²⁵The day of the birth of Mahdi, the Twelfth Imam of the Ithna'ashari (Ja'fari) Shi'is, in the Islamic lunar calendar. (tr)

²⁶<u>'Ajam</u> is an Arabic term used by both Arabs and Iranians to refer to an Iranian or a barbarian, or often someone who is both, as in this situation. (tr)

²⁷*I'm quoting the oral version I heard from Isma'il Ra'in, my dear friend who lives in that area.* (A)

²⁸*Khalil Maleki noticed this 'facelessness' in our young people sooner than any of the rest of us. See the weekly publication <u>Mehregan</u> for the years 32,33,34 [1964-66], and later on in the magazine '<u>Elm ow Zendegi</u> [Knowledge and Life] for the years 38-39 [1966-69] in repeated articles on the same subject.* (A)

²⁹*As used here, the term Shu'ubi refers not only to the Shu'ubites but to any political or religious campaign in which the central issue is the supremacy of the Persians over the Arabs.* (tr)

³⁰*The Shah's radio disputes with the religious leaders (Esfand '41-Farvardin '42 [late Jan-early April 1963]) made the truth of this prediction's claims apparent. And then the merciless massacre of the fifteenth of Khordad 1342 [June 5, 1963], which even Radio Moscow denounced as a reactionary uprising! And rejoiced!* (A)

³¹*And from the above date on it has overtly oppressed it, when both the monarchy and religion are centuries-old holdovers from the past. And in any case there are no two institutions that need each other so much. The important thing is that this confrontation between the two rivals after three hundred years of suppressing differences is again coming out into the open. This is clearly the beginning of a new phase, the beginning of a phase in which the spread of education and the expansion of intellectualism will surround these two rivals. This confrontation led to the Shah's assassination in Mirza*

Shirazi's time, and it led to the ouster of Mohammad
'Ali Shah and a change of regime in the time of the
Constitutional Revolution. What will it lead to
today? Well, this is a problem for the intellectuals. (A)

        ³²This reclamation never actually took place.
(tr)

        ³³Two or three Swedish academics are preparing
linguistic atlases of Iran and Afghanistan. Good
news? Or bad news? In any case the one for Afghanistan has been completed but the one for Iran is
still unfinished--for reasons not appropriate for
discussion here. (A)

        ³⁴I want to draw assistance once again from the
French researcher Rene Grousset from that same book
The Face of Asia, p. 132:

        "In the uprising Iran staged against the oil
company, affirmation and praise arose from Aghanis-
tan, Pakistan, and the Arab League simultaneously.
This was the first time that Iranian Shi'ism, which
throughout all these centuries had been like a dam
blocking cooperation among Islamic nations, joined
the Islamic unity. And why? Because the time had
passed when the Safavid Shahs and the defenders of
Shi'ism were compelled to unite with Europe against
the Ottoman Sultan, who was the Sunni Caliph."

        I say the Europeans retracted their horns. In
any case, is this good news for us Asians of the
Middle East? Or a danger signal from the petroleum
consortium, in which the French don't have such a big
share? In any case, what I have quietly suggested
over and over again--this gentleman has stated more
clearly. (A)

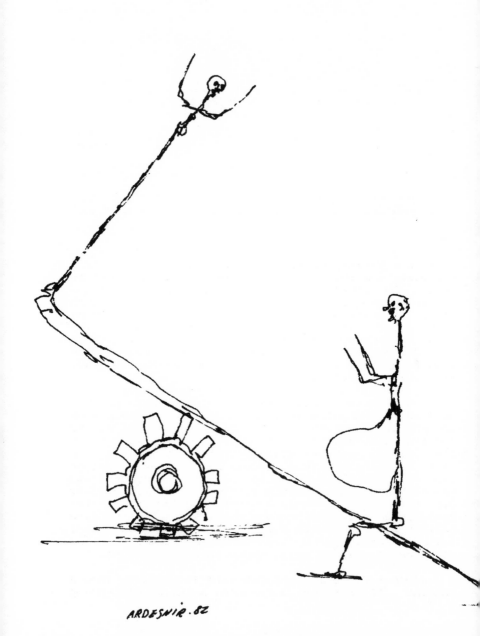

ARDESNIR.82

6

BREAKING THE TALISMAN'S SPELL

As a growing nation, we have now stood to face machines and technology, and without much determination. In other words, we've decided to accept whatever comes. What should we do about this? Should we continue to be mere consumers as we have been in the past? Should we close the doors of our lives to machines and technology and withdraw into the distant past, with national *and religious* traditions? Or is there a third alternative? We'll deal with these questions one by one.

Until now, the course we've taken is to be mere consumers of machines and to simply submit ourselves to the fate of the twentieth century. That course has led us to this current situation, a Weststruck situation in which we await Western alternatives in a daze, waiting for them to come and give us credit or aid every few years so we can buy their products and replace worn-out machinery. *This is really an easy way to go, and the cause of laziness, indolence, incompetence, and idleness,* but if this process were getting us anywhere we wouldn't have all this chaos *and be so emperiled by bankruptcy,* and at least there would be no need to write these things.

Even a frivolous cricket doesn't withdraw into a cocoon. If nothing else we're a nation undergoing change. If our values and our thinking have come into a state of turmoil, it's because we're shaking off our old crust. Perhaps we're awaiting permission to enter the new age. It's the awe of machines that's making us shake so much. Suppose it weren't this way. Suppose we remained prejudiced and bound to tradition, living the primitive life of the dawn of creation, the way most of our villagers do now. Isn't it true that we'd be forced by political and economic necessity *and our common interests with other segments of humanity* to give over half our land to the picks and shovels of foreign companies, so they could come here and dig, excavate, extract, and remove? How long can we sit beside the road and watch the caravan go by? *Or sit beside the creek and watch life go by?* Even Ibn Sa'ud, living with his pre-Islamic prejudices, *who still chops off heads and hands* [and] /still cut off Abu Talib Yazdi's head,/[1] has accepted the changes that come with machines.

A third alternative, however, which cannot be avoided, is to put the genie of machines back in his bottle and make him work for us, like a beast of burden. Machines are a natural springboard for us, one that we must use to make the longest possible leap. We must adopt machines, but we must not remain slaves to them. We must not become entangled with them. Machines are a means, not an end. *The aim is to eliminate poverty and to see to the spiritual and material welfare of all of humanity.*

When horses were our means of transportation, we had fields and pastures, all of them green and flourishing, where we bred the most beautiful horses of the noblest stock. We had branding places, where we placed upon them the mark of human ownership. We had stables for them where they could train, rest, and breed. We had caravanserais where we could get fresh horses. We had races and galloping shooting matches to exercise the muscles of animals and human beings. Is a machine any different than a horse, which is tamed by people in order to serve them? If we, as human beings, had nothing to do with the original genetic formation of horses, the embryo of a machine is fashioned by humans from the cylinders and the *pistons* outward.

We must first have an *economy* appropriate for machines--*an independent economy*--and also training, classes, and procedures. Then we'll need a furnace to melt the steel and shape it according to human in-

[handwritten left margin: This really romanticizes the old]

[handwritten bottom: So solution prof talked about?]

tention, then specialists who can modify it and shape
it in various ways, then schools that can teach these
specialties in a practical way, then factories where
the steel can be transformed into machines, *and other
manufactures*, and then markets in the cities and villages where the machines *and other manufactures* can
be made available to the people....

Don't ask me to go into further detail, for this
is not within my competence and it's out of bounds
for these pages. It's imperative to make machines in
order to control them. That which is made by other
hands, even if it be an amulet or talisman to ward
off jealous eyes, will certainly contain unknown elements from fearsome worlds beyond the reach of human
influence, with some secret embedded in them. The
one who possesses that amulet or talisman doesn't own
it. *Rather, he is in a sense the property of the
talisman, because he* lives in the shadow of its
protection, always with the danger and fear that he
may insult the talisman, that the sky may see its
color,² or that he may drop it on the ground.

But if a child who has this very talisman around
his neck *should get older* and happen to curiously
unwrap it to see what it is, and especially if he's
able to look at it and see the triangles, rectangles,
stars, and pompous language written on its oily
paper, and if he's able to understand the meaning of
the words, ideas, and figures--*or their
meaninglessness*--would there any longer be any fear
of it in his heart? Machines are talismans for us
Weststruck folk. We drag ourselves into the shadow
of their protection, and in their shelter we think
ourselves immune to the evils of the time, oblivious
of the fact that this is a talisman others have hung
around our necks to intimidate and milk us. Let's be
curious--*let's grow up a little*--and ultimately
unwrap this talisman *and obtain its secret*.

/Well and good./ *Of course one may ask*, if the
solution is so easy, then why hasn't it occurred to
our nation's thinkers? Or if it has occurred to
them, why hasn't the business of unwrapping this
talisman gotten under way physically? In answering
these two questions I will name only two of the
causes. You can guess the rest of them for yourselves. Definitely, the first reason is that fear and
respect are still in our hearts. We know that the
words <u>haram</u> [forbidden] and <u>tahrim</u> [forbid] come from
the same root as the words <u>ehteram</u> [respect] and <u>hor-</u>

mat [honor]. Fear of machines is the same thing as
the fear of talismans. If it's forbidden for us to
touch or unwrap a talisman, we're also forbidden to
perceive the secrets of machines or to understand
them. God knows that this fear has caused
Gharbzadegi, or else that Gharbzadegi produced fear
in us born of respect. It's like the case of the
chicken and the egg.

Forget that. Consider instead the fact that
we're still living in the days of Ali Baba and the
Forty Thieves of Baghdad. We stood behind a wall or
looked through a keyhole and saw the thieves come.
They pronounced a formulation or repeated an incantation three times and the wall opened up just like a
door, and what a treasure was concealed behind that
door! We still put our best efforts into imitating
the incantations of those thieves. We worked hard
and learned the incantation, repeated it like par-
rots, and the wall opened, but *the libertines* had
taken the treasure! As soon as we forget the temptation of that treasure and concentrate instead on what
made the wall open, on the secret of its movement and
how the incantation affected it, we'll have found a
practical procedure and will be capable of unraveling the talisman of machines.

Our current situation is such that we use
machines from morning to night. We even cook our
meals on them every day. Yet we're just like a child
whose mother frightens him by putting a pot over her
head pretending to be a demon--machines intimidate us
in exactly the same way. They're like that demon
who's really only the child's everyday soup pot and
his very mother who shelters him in her warm embrace.
It is because of this fear--*or because the country
has no framework to support 'technicians'' demands*--
that most of our college students in Europe study
either medicine, psychology, or something else in the
humanities. It is due to this very fear that we have
so many agricultural engineers who are now land as-
sessors in the Mortgage [Rahni] Bank, so many
chemists working as director generals, and so many
mineralogists who are contractors.

It's true that we've wearied the minds and
thoughts of the people's children for years in our
schools with chemical, physical, and mathematical
formulas and equations, and that we've almost
eliminated literature, philosophy, and ethics from
all our high schools and colleges. The mind of every

secondary school graduate is a repository of laws, formulas, and equations, but to what purpose? There's no practical setting for the hypotheses and equations. We haven't put theory into practice for the students in any laboratory. We're still obliged to turn to some European laboratory to measure every rock, earth sample, and batch of tar!

It's strange that we, who are so attentive to detail in our traditional crafts--in carpet weaving, tile making, and inlay work--are so careless when it comes to machines, but it's not surprising. *Don't you think that* this carelessness with machines, technology, and the new sciences is the result of our confidence that our oil fields will produce indefinitely? And in machines that must come *as a requirement* in exchange for petroleum *money* and credit? /You see that we've returned to the fundamental cause, which is that we've been satisfied to be mere consumers of machines./

Most interesting of all, I've heard that some of our national leaders are even 'theorizing' on these matters. "Yes," they say, "now that we're a petroleum-rich nation and the Westerner is giving us everything from chicken milk to human souls in exchange for this petroleum on a silver platter, why should we trouble ourselves? Why bother with building factories and heavy industries and their entanglements, such as training specialists, tolerating the junk the industries produce when they're getting started, coming to grips with the grievances of labor, management, insurance, pensions, and so on...." And in fact this is exactly how we do things. This same new theory has been the operating principle in these provinces for years. And this very thing is one of the reasons for our Gharbzadegi. *Or one of the fundamental results of it. We're back to that story of the chicken and the egg again.*

And then again, if we're exacting with our *elegant national and local arts and not in our work with machines, it's because* those arts have been passed on orally from breast to breast. For years fathers have passed an art on to sons in the workshop, and apprentice and master have worked together. We've had professional, *practical, and theoretical* training *to an extent that training in these elegant arts has acquired traditions, principles, and fine points,* and harkens back to the depths of the years. But machines are newcomers to

the scene. They have no tradition. There is no
training or classroom instruction for them. The
stages of apprenticeship and journeyman status have
yet to be established.

In a situation /like ours,/ it's to be expected
that if we build a big dam or if our oil well (meaning their oil well) catches fire we have to run to
some foreign expert or specialist who has more experience and background than we have. But the pity
is that not only do we refer to foreign experts in
exceptional instances such as this, but we do it for
a great many other things as well. In order to assemble a cement factory, a sugar refinery, a tire
retreading factory(!) or a textile or cord mill, not
only do we still import all the machines intact from
Europe and America, but along with the machines we
also bring a crew that's Western from top to bottom,
from the unskilled laborers to the engineer and chief
engineer, with astronomical salaries. Then we host
them for three, four, or ten years in some area where
they are given free rein everywhere, so the cement
furnace will glow, the sugar will be pure, and the
wool will be made into strong thread. Of course, if
we're precise about it, this isn't surprising either.
We either don't have anyone else besides these
people, or if we do have them it's useless because
those who sell us a factory write it into the sales
agreement that they will guarantee its proper performance only after their specialists have assembled
it and transferred it. Yes, this is the fate of a
backward, Weststruck economy. If you can do any better, build your own factory. If you want to assemble
it, build it yourself. If I build it, I want to send
my engineer somewhere along with the machine: on a
trip to the sunny South, for vacation and recreation,
for a new experience, greater experimental latitude,
and a broader perspective in this world of machine
consumers!

As for the second cause, it arises out of what
I've said already, or is an accessory to it. It is
that as long as we're purchasers of Western industrial products the seller will be unwilling to
give up such an acquiescent customer. It is that we
are only buyers in this mercantile world--or just
consumers--and that the builder, who's also the
seller, knows the tricks of his trade and how to ar-
range things so that this disproportion will remain
forever stable and that there won't ever be any conflict in this buyer-seller relationship. Therefore,

it's only fair that the West should have the right to withhold permission *(meaning credit)*, or to consistently obstruct our becoming machine manufacturers. This very West, *which has our governments making claims to democracy and having a heterosexual Majlis for its benefit,* /installs and removes our governments, helps us stay on our feet, adjusts the load we carry as if we were pack mules,/sets up conventions of orientalists for us, and *regularly* pats our leaders on the back on its radio programs and in its newspapers *once a week or once a month. After all, they've heard that the nation is deeply under the European spell!* /Anyway, India wants to stand on her own two feet, the Chinese market is closed to the West except for England, and if we became manufacturers of machines they'd have nothing left./

From the point of view of the economic profit of the big Western manufacturers--meaning from the point of view of the international economy(!)--the later we turn our hands to machines and technology the better! *UNESCO says the same thing too, and acts on it, as does ICAFE, the FAO, and the UN itself as well!* All our ruinations and chaos have their origins in this point, *in the fact that in world affairs they've compelled us to look out for the interests of the economy of the machine manufacturers.*

If our politics have been generally a function of variables in the West over the last two-hundred years, it's because during this period our economy has been a function of those same variables. I believe I've given an example of this from the petroleum situation. The exception is the one or two years between 1950 and 1953 *(Dr. Mossadeq's government)* when we even exported beans.[3] *At that time the guiding principle of the country's economic management had nothing to to with petroleum revenue. And how appropriate that was. And this is something that could be resumed again at any time. But as long as the petroleum wheel turns on the strength of credit from its revenues and on the fostering of parasites, the situation will remain just as it is.[4]* /Look at the situation now. A kilo of pistachios that cost thirty tumans [$4.20] two years ago can now be had for eight tumans [$1.15] less. What do we really have besides gum tragacinth, a bit of cotton, carpets, and oil-bearing seed? Other than petroleum./Petroleum that the West itself exploits, itself refines, itself transports, itself accounts for financially, and our annual petroleum royalties (forty million pounds sterling or so), which the West itself deposits in its national banks as credit towards purchases of its industrial production. We're *inevitably* obliged, in order to use this credit, to buy from this same *'itself'*. Who is this *'itself'*? Forty percent of it is America and her satellitess, another forty percent England and her supporters, and the remainder France, Holland, or others like them. We must import machines in place of this oil they take out. *And after the machines, specialists, and after the specialists, machines: specialists in dialects, literature, painting, and musicians!* This is why /Richfield/ and Morrison-Knudsen can bring anything they want from America, *from bulldozers to cable, bolts, and nuts,* and A.G.I.P. Mineraria imports without restriction from Italy, John Molem *the road builder* from England, and Entrepose from France.

More interesting is the undercover dealing that *goes on in the midst of all this. John Molem caused a scandal and gathered up his gear and left, but he isn't a quitter, and he's still at it just the same. Where?* At Time magazine, and he's propagandizing for the head of the Planning and Budget Organization, who helped him get his foot in the door over here.[5] *And who was the Tehran chief of this John Molem? Mr. Peter Avery, the English Farsi-speaking orientalist, a very charming and likeable person and a teacher of Eastern(!) languages at Cambridge and [the University of] Michigan! I went to see him at Cambridge, in the winter of 1341 [1963]. He had wanted to see me. The lady that was my hostess had put a visit with him on the schedule. I put a copy of the first edition of this very booklet under my arm and went to find him. Come in, and talk, chatter, and hospitality.* In the course of discussing other matters I said to him: "You know, Sir(!) Edward Browne didn't become who he was by becoming chief of John Molem when he was in Tehran!" *He started sobbing.* "He had money and wealth, and I was poor."

From this exchange I realized that people are *equally diminutive the world over. Then this same man has recently written a book called* Modern Iran *in which he dealt with me in this way:*

> Recently a book appeared about the 'disease' of Westernism. It was, incidentally, banned by the authorities. Men who think like its author are probably a minority among educated

Table 1.
Ten-Year Table of Exports and Imports, 1331-40
(From Iran Almanac 1963, p. 293, Printed in Tehran).

Years	Imports		Exports	
	Weight (Tons)	Rials (Thousands)	Weight (Tons)	Rials (Thousands)
(1331) 1952-53	232,236	5,031,394	354,079	5,831,528
1953-54	424,445	5,424,266	443,764	8,425,622
1954-55	503,226	7,225,015	490,478	10,288,171
1955-56	637,132	9,125,439	507,873	8,033,726
1956-57	744,876	20,981,288	463,529	7,930,690
1957-58	743,784	25,129,342	436,641	8,352,922
1958-59	986,092	33,458,260	445,398	7,940,615
1959-60	1,201,950	41,630,135	397,231	7,701,017
1960-61	1,913,514	52,657,139	446,307	8,359,870
(1340) 1961-62	1,619,234	47,170,707	551,384	9,593,450

Subtract the figures from each other for yourselves. I'm ashamed to do it.
Instead I'll quote an item from the introduction to the magazine Bank-e Melli-
ye Iran [National Bank of Iran], no. 254, by Mr. Kvosh Kish, one of the bank's
experts:

"For a period of almost thirty-two years only twelve banks with several
branches have been active in Iran, five of which were specialized banks.
But in the years 1335 to 1339 [1956-61] (the period of the open door
policy), in only three years fourteen new banks with several branches and
representatives and agents were established.... Their function is to pay
salaries to workers in foreign factories whose merchandise we have purchased. In the six-year period between 1332 and 1339 [1953-1961] the
volume of our imports has necessarily gone from seven billion rials to
fifty-two billion six-hundred million rials, or approximately an eight-
fold increase." [Translators' note: 70 Rials = $1.00.]

Iranians, but history shows that no intellectual movement in Iran, however small its
beginnings, can be totally ignored.',⁷

Yes. These gentlemen are wary of affairs in
this way. Or Ford and Rockefeller's companies have
their cultural foundations, and they give grants to
this one and that one for the expansion of education.
Very good. Relying on these very funds, the Iran
Foundation goes and builds a hospital and a university in Shiraz; but go see what sanctuaries they've
built for the nobility, how the official language of
their college of literature is Engrish [sic], right
next to Hafez and Sa'di, and see what an observatory
they've built to study the movements of American
satellites and how they've imported everything from
the nuts and bolts to the pots and burners and doors
and frames from America!

Or this same Ford and Rockefeller give money to
Franklin [Book Programs] in Tehran to furnish the
schools with books. Go see it.' What huge companies have built it and what a textbook monopoly
they've made. And how they've broken the back of
every local publisher!

We had gone to Firuzabad (on Nawruz of 1341 [Mar
21 1963] with Mohandes Seyhun, Farrokh Gaffari, and
Mohandes Moqtader) Kazerun, and Shiraz to spend some
time in the desert. We heard that in Shapur near
Kazerun His Excellency Mr. [Roman] Ghirshman was
working on his excavations. We said let's go say
hello and look around. But he wasn't there. Or if
he was he was asleep and wouldn't receive us. But
his tent and shed were right there at Shapur-e
Kazerun, and the petroleum consortium's marks and
emblems were everywhere, on the tents, the materials,
and the machines. What does this mean? It means
that the excavations of the archaeologists at Shapur-
e Kazerun are the progeny of the petroleum industry!
And this is how it is that his excellency
Mr. Ghirshman wants to prove by force of bombast that
Khark [Island] was a Christian community, among other
things....'

/Yes, this is give-and-take, or compulsory
barter./ This is the way petroleum goes out and
machines come in, with all their baggage, from orientalists and specialists to films, literature, and
books. /Who profits from this give-and-take?/ The
first ones are the manufacturing companies, for whom

*the profits of all investments outside their own
country are tax-exempt*, and then the middlemen. Who
are these middlemen? /You know better than I do./[10]
*Other than the ones I've mentioned, guess who they
are for yourselves...* This is the reason we have
ministers, parliamentary representatives, why our
governments are shaken up in the aftermath of these
transactions, and cabinets come and go.

Our politicians are led just this way by the
West, while the West secretly undermines them, or
gives them its praise, and it's no wonder our political leaders give more credence to what Reuter and UPI
or *Time* have to say than to the Chamber of Commerce
of Tehran, the Planning Commission of the Ministry of
Education, or the City Council of Birjland. If that
city has such a council. When the country's economy
is in other people's hands and those other people
build machines, it's clear that we must always be
needy purchasers. Fortunately [for them], the payments on these bulldozers and tractors out /in these
bare deserts/ have not even ended /before the
machines themselves swallow that last cup of li-
quefied dung,/ *rusted and collapsed.* And the companies only guarantee them for five years![11]

*What's interesting in this regard is when they
have a confrontation of some kind somewhere in the
world. This becomes the top story for UPI and
Reuters. Then the Red Cross will start crying that
two of its nurses, for example, were wounded, and the
foreigners living there pack up their travel bags.
Then the pope in Rome prays that the calamity in that
part of the world be relieved. Then prices plummet
on the London and New York stock exchanges. Then the*
Times *and the* New York Times *start writing two-faced
articles showing the ins and outs of the factors at
work in the region. Then they sever political relations. Then mercenary soldiers are everywhere and
the Seventh Fleet starts maneuvering in the Mediterranean or in the Persian Gulf, or off the coast of
China or Africa. We've experienced these things a
number of times. With the nationalization of oil,
with the Suez Canal, in Cuba, the Congo, and Vietnam.*

In fairness, however, it must be said that our
economists and politicians aren't idle in the midst
of this. *Weststruck economists will sit and talk,
foreign consultants will come and go, and suddenly
you see a Jeep or a Fiat assembly plant being built,
or a plastics factory or battery plant for the mili-*

tary going up and several military officers in prison
for corruption. And all this with such grandeur and
ceremony, and scissors, three-colored ribbons, and
pomp. But what's the truth of the matter? The truth
is it's no longer profitable for the companies to
send even calico, silk, batteries, and unbreakable
aftabehs[12] to us. It's to their own advantage to export only heavy machinery. And then if a foreign
company can export various components of a machine as
parts, the import duties will be less, the expense of
packing and transport will be lower, and of course
the labor costs of assembling those parts in a
country such as Iran are lower than those in Europe
and the United States. This is why such a hot market
has grown up in the developing countries for assembly
plants for Jeeps, Fiats, radios, batteries, and other
rootless ancillary industries. Let's not forget, of
course, that this is a step forward in any case for a
backward country, and if it isn't a proper and well-
considered step, at least it can be used for display,
and after all, an official report can be issued every
year that says, "yes, this year there was so much
percent increase in the number of workers, the amount
of national capital investment, and in foreign investment."[13]

        And after we discuss these things we hold semi-
nars, devise scenarios for [development] Plans Two
and Three,[14] hold commissions, and there's a never-
ending stream of advisors coming in and going out.
And in any event, assembling a machine is something
like repair work. It's not an industry, and it's not
building machines. If you want the truth, however,
these things are all accessories to Western industry.

        Let's especially keep it in mind that if there's
a need for a Second and Third Plan, and if the World
Bank and public opinion in the Western nations(!) is
applying pressure, it means that when the company
managers permit a government in Iran to have plans
that are superficially more modern, broader, longer
term, and more diversified, it's mainly because
Western industry must know how much of its industrial
production Iran can absorb during the next five
years, and what kind of capacity and tolerance it
will have as a buyer. They don't do things spontaneously the way we do. Everything is done according to plan. We know that surplus production brings
crisis, activates the monster of unemployment, and
intensifies the danger of a change of regime in those
nations. After all, His Excellency Mr. [Charles] De

Table 2.

Province	Industrial Units	Workers	Capital Investment Thousands of Rials
West Azarbaijan	152	2,676	902,473
Kermanshah	366	4,062	844,373
Khuzestan	272	3,044	1,465,025
Fars	347	4,642	1,987,831
Kerman	208	1,963	682,093
Khorasan	843	11,069	3,278,087
Esfahan	899	24,006	5,842,838
Sistan va Baluchestan	89	304	62,010
Tehran	2,844	48,556	22,297,274
Gilan	856	7,659	2,802,233
Mazandaran	883	16,504	4,621,189
East Azarbaijan	393	6,229	728,363
Total	8,156	130,714	45,513,789

This means that the number of workers in the country's entire population is 130,000 as opposed to a population of twenty million!

Gaulle has high hopes still,[1] Mr. [Harold] Macmillan
has not yet reached retirement age, and President
[John F.] Kennedy is still in the prime of his youth.
No matter what happens, the West must know how much
it can milk this quiet, acquiescent customer during
the term of the Third Plan, and what percentage of
its petroleum royalties to retain and exchange for
refrigerators, radios, and pressure cookers.

We know that the principal overseers of all
those committees, seminars, and educational and industrial consultants are Westerners,[1] *with precise
intentions and specific goals.* Don't talk to me
about *the impartiality and high-mindedness of* those
UN and UNESCO advisors. Not even the gold and
diamond-mining companies of the Congo paid any attention to their late Secretary General Hammarskjold.
We saw how that respected body came to the defense
there of these same Belgian and English gold- and
diamond-mining companies. The Iranians, of course,
also participate in these seminars and planning committees, which means that our top intellectuals are
our most Weststruck people. But how do they participate? I'm very sorry if this is insulting, but I
don't think the Iranian participants in these planning seminars ever get beyond the status of interpreters! If they did surpass that role and *express
an opinion, first, it wouldn't be acceptable, and
second,* they'd forfeit the right to sit with the big
shots.

If our politics and economy, to the extent that
we've seen, are functions of the West's politics and
economy, and if we're so Weststruck, it's because
most of our intellectuals--those who've gained a
foothold in the country's leadership machinery--in
the last analysis, and [supposedly] as the most ex-
alted mission of conscience and perception, are
interpreters for Western advisors. They're agents
and interpreters of their views and intentions. But
don't we already know how many thousand dry ganats
and how many thousand unemployed, illiterate, and
uneducated people we have with no health
facilities?[1] This is no reason to go running to
foreign consultants and advisors every minute. I
wish our dependence on them could untie just one knot
for us, /and that it weren't such a failure and
didn't always fall flat on its face. Read one of the
books by Millspaugh,[1] who had the run of our nation's economy at one time, and you'll see that he
committed every possible absurdity and that his dis-

graces were countless./

/I wish all the advisors had been like Millspaugh, who didn't have such a vast entourage of Weststruck intellectuals in his service./ *I wish a day would come when we wouldn't need this troop of consultants and advisors.* Today, it's because we're dependent on these very intellectuals participating in the government that the West's political representatives and advisors treat us the same way the Russian and British ambassadors treated Atabak[19] and Amir Kabir,[20] assuming one would want to put our Weststruck intellectuals in the same league with these two great figures. Furthermore, if only ambassadors imposed their opinions on us in those days, now there are legions of Western advisors, parasites, specialists, and experts. If they only directed their persuasive efforts towards Atabak and Amir Kabir in those days, both of whom were world-wise old men experienced in their own Eastern way of life, traditions, and criteria and bound by the constraints of the beliefs, ceremonies, and formalities of this side of the world, now there's a whole group of Weststruck intellectuals on the side of the West's dialogue and opinion who have neither the capability of Atabak and Amir Kabir, nor even that of Hajji Mirza Aqasi,[21] *and I don't know why he's been erroneously branded as an incompetent.*[22]

This is the way they run a nation, a nation abandoned to the fate of machines, guided by these Weststruck intellectuals, in the hands of these seminars, conferences, Second and Third Plans, and relying on foreign aid 'handouts' *and this ridiculous investment in rootless ancillary industries.*

We've said enough about machine destiny. Now we see what kind of people these national leaders are—these /old men, young men, and/ Weststruck intellectuals. True, these are generalizations, but you can separate out the exceptions for yourselves.

NOTES

[1]Abu Talib Yazdi was an Iranian Muslim who was executed by the Saudi Arabian government by order of King Ibn Sa'ud for the crime of desecration, which he committed while circumambulating the __Kaaba__ inside the Grand Mosque in Mecca. He vomited on the sacred soil after being overcome by heat exhaustion and just before passing out. The incident produced friction between Iran and Saudi Arabia and resulted in a temporary ban on trips to Mecca, ordered by the shah. (tr)

[2]The author refers here to a type of amulet consisting of cryptic writings on a small piece of paper which is folded, placed inside a series of small boxes, and tightly wrapped. The mullah who prepares it typically enjoins the user not to allow the sky to see the color of the writing or to drop it. (tr)

[3]A reference to domestic economic gains made during the so-called "oil-less economy." See Cottam, op. cit., p. 200. (tr)

[4]*See table 1.* (A)

[5]*See the American __Time__ magazine. February 28, 1964, p. 40, last column, concerning Mr. Ebtehaj.* (A)

[6]*Modern Iran. By Peter Avery. Ed. Ernest Benn. London, 1965, p.468*(A)

[7]We have taken this passage directly from Avery's book. Al-e Ahmad's Farsi translation differs in that the Farsi term for __unfortunately__ appears where __incidentally__ should have been, and it does not use quotation marks for the word __disease.__ (tr)

[8]*See "Belbeshu-ye Ketabha-ye Darsi"* [The Confusion in Textbooks] *in __Seh Maqaleh-ye Digar__* [Three more articles], *by this writer.* (A)

[9]*See __Jazireh-ye Khark__, by this writer, and also the pamphlet this same Ghirshman wrote about the island. And remember that it was one of these very*

orientalists/archaeologists who discovered the presence of oil in Khuzestan. Meaning the Frenchman [Jacques Jean Marie] *de Morgan, who had come to Iran even before D'Arcy to excavate in Susa. The results of his excavations were published in the Journal of Mines* [Annales des Mines] *printed in Paris, and what an uproar, and so on.... See Panjah Sal-e Naft Dar Iran* [Fifty years of petroleum in Iran] *(Tehran: 1956 or 7) by Mustafa Fatih.* (A)

[10]A veiled reference to the royal family et al. (tr)

[11]*The Lebanese philosopher Charles* [Habib] *Malik, former president of the United Nations General Assembly, accused Western capitalists of having nothing in their bags for the developing nations except material goods. He also said, "Roads, dams, efficiency, and the smile of rulers--that is all that matters: But spirit, freedom, joy, happiness, truth, man--that never enters the mind. A world of perfect technicians is the aim, not a world of human beings, let alone of beings divine." Translated from page 77 of this same American Time magazine, September* [27] *1963 from the report on talks at the thirteenth International Management Conference. This conference was held in Manhattan, attended by 4,200 people from eighty-four countries.* (A) [Translators' note: Malik's remarks appeared in Time as we have given them here. Al-e Ahmad's Farsi translation is again quite loose, but not significantly different in meaning. One might note his substitution of "these are the things that are imposed upon the backward nations" for "that is all that matters."]

[12]An aftabeh is any long-spouted pitcher kept in a privy to provide water for washing the body's excreting orifices. Due to its obvious hygienic superiority, its use is much preferred throughout the Middle East to the "toilet paper" to which Westerners are accustomed. (tr)

[13]*The numbers of workers and the industrial capital installations in which they work are shown in Table 2. (from p. 405 of the Iran Almanac of 1963, printed in Tehran).* (A)

[14]Referring to the Second and Third Plans of the Pahlavi regime's five successive five-year economic development plans. (tr)

¹⁵*Remember that the first edition of this book
was published in Mehr of 1341* [Sep 23-Oct 22 1962]
(A)

¹⁶*We don't have statistics and official figures,
but it is said that there are now (1341 [1962])
thirty-thousand foreign experts, engineers, and
specialists working in this country.* (A)

¹⁷*I'll cite some official figures as an example.:
Currently, in the health field, we need 9,500
physicians while we have only 5,915. Of the 3,800
needed medical assistants and midwives, we have only
1,000 people. We have only 19,327 hospital beds out
of the 190,000 we need. In education we had only
4,277 people with teaching degrees at the beginning
of the 1340/1961 academic year to fill 9,485 positions. /In 1310/1931 the first group of graduates of
the National Teacher's College numbered only fifteen
as opposed to 300 high school graduates, and in
1340/1961 the same National Teacher's College
graduated 270 people as opposed to fourteen- to
sixteen- thousand high school graduates, meaning the
certified teachers have multiplied some eighteen
times while the high school graduates have multiplied
some forty-seven times. Many statistics of this nature may be cited./ For example, of the fifty-
thousand villages in this country, only seven-
thousand of them have schools. An interesting piece
of news is that with all our cultural poverty, in the
year 1342* [Mar 21 1963 - Mar 20 1964] *they closed all
the higher and junior-level teachers' colleges in the
country on the grounds that boarding schools are a
superfluous expense, and so on... This is how 42
teachers' colleges across the country were closed.*
(A)

¹⁸Arthur Millspaugh, financial advisor to Reza
Shah, and author of __Americans in Persia__ (Washington,
D.C.: The Brookings institute, 1946) and __The American
Task in Persia__ (New York, London: Century, 1925).
See also Cottam, op. cit., pp. 207-208. (tr)

¹⁹Atabak, prime minister under Muhammad 'Ali
Shah (1907-1909). See Cottam, op. cit., pp. 47-49.
(tr)

²⁰Mirza Taqi Khan Amir Kabir, prime minister
under Nasir od-Din Shah (1848-1851). See Hamid Algar, __Religion and State in Iran, 1785-1906__ (Berkeley:
1969), chapters 7 and 9. (tr)

¹¹Hajji Mirza Aqasi, prime minister and spiritual preceptor to Muhammad Shah (1834-1848), remembered for his political inanity. See ibid., chapter 6. (tr)

¹¹'Abd Allah Mustawfi has defended this old man in *Sharh-e Hal-e Zendegi-ye Man* [My autobiography (Tehran: 'Elmi, 1945)] (pp. 45-50) and has shown that it was [Mirza Abu-l-Qasim] *Qa'im Maqam's* grudge against him that created this reputation. (A)

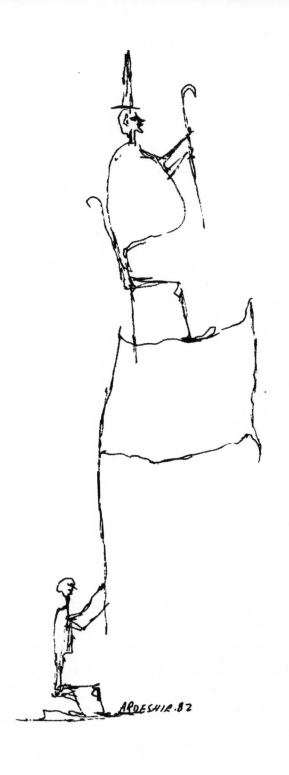

7

A DONKEY IN A LION'S SUIT
OR A LION ON A FLAG?

A Weststruck person who's a part of our national
leadership apparatus has his feet in the air. He's a
particle of dust suspended in space, just like straw
floating on water. He's cut his ties with the core
of society, culture, and tradition. It's not like
having no relationship between the ancient and the
modern nor like a transitional line between the old
and the new. This is a phenomenon with no
relationship to the past and no perception of the future. It's not a point along any line. It's some
imaginary point on a page, or perhaps in space, just
like that suspended particle of dust.

Inevitably you ask, "How did this man emerge as
leader of the country?" I say it happened because of
the exigencies of machines, and the fate of a political policy that has no choice but to follow the
policies of the big powers. On this side of the
world, *and especially in the petroleum-rich nations,*
it's customary for whatever is inconsequential to
rise to the top of the water. The tide of events *in
petroleum repositories of this nature* washes only
sticks and straw to the surface. It lacks the
strength to reach down to bottom of the sea and toss
pearls ashore. We, in our <u>Gharbzadegi</u> and the pains
arising from it, are stuck with this insubstantial
drifter on the waves of events, the ordinary blame-

less man on the street, who can't be criticized, *to whom no one listens and who's* done nothing wrong. He'll go wherever you send him, meaning that he'll become anything you train him to be.[2]

The plain truth of the matter is that this man on the street has no control over his own destiny, and we neither ask him nor consult with him in order to determine his destiny. We ask the *foreign* consultants and advisors instead. Things are that bad. We're that entangled with Weststruck *leaders,* only some of whom have studied, and sometimes been to Europe and America.

I wish our involvement with the country's Weststruck leadership were limited to those people who have been educated in the West, but it really isn't. Very confidentially, the way I see it is that, due to the demands of *these very things,* these same /machines, policies, and economic principles,/ in the provinces on this side of the world it's the custom for every group and trade to be run by <u>lumpens.</u> /Excuse me for using a foreign expression. I can't be explicit./ *Meaning the failures, those who have no ability, the listless.* The most unreliable tradesmen are the ones who run the bazaars and the chamber of commerce. The most inept educators are the educational executives. The bankowners are the most bankrupt *moneychangers* of all. Those among us who *are the most useless,* or who most resemble dangerous unchained animals, are representatives in the assembly. The most muddleheaded people are the nation's leaders. *As I said,* separate out the exceptions for yourselves.

The usual practice in this country is to confer power on those who are rootless and *without personality,* if not on the ruthless and the corrupt. There's no place in this setup for the one who rightfully belongs there, who speaks the truth, sees accurately, and does the right thing. If we're to do a good job of following the West, someone must lead the nation who's *easily led,* who isn't genuine, *who's unprincipled,* has no roots, and is not of the soil of this land. This is why our Weststruck leader floats with the tide, unanchored anywhere. This is why his position is never clear. He can't commit himself to any issue or problem. He's confused. He shifts position constantly. He has no inner direction. He moves with the tide of events. He can never take issue with anything. He flatters and cajoles his way

around the biggest rock. No crisis or turn of events
seems dangerous to him. *If this government goes
there's always the next one. If he doesn't get on
this committee he'll be on that seminar. If not in
this newspaper, then on television. If he's not in
this office he'll be in that ministry. If not ambas-
sador, then minister.* The government, therefore, may
come and go a thousand times, but you'll always see
these same Weststruck leaders planted as solidly as
Mount Uhud.[3]

        This Weststruck man is also sneaky, because at
least he knows what part of the world he's living in.
He knows it's stifling here. He knows the wind blows
in a different direction every day. He doesn't need
a compass to locate the poles of power. Consequently, he's everywhere. In the political parties, in
society, in the newspapers, /in the Writer's Association,/ in the government, /in seminars,/ in the
Educational Commission, in the /Consultative/ Assembly /and the Senate,/ and in the Contractors' Union.
In order to be everywhere he must be with everyone.
To be with everyone he must *be tactful and* please
everyone, *and not be muleheaded.* He is, therefore,
submissive and ready to go. He's complacent, and
sometimes he writes articles against rocking the
boat.[4] He mustn't be ignorant of philosophy and has
to talk about freedom too. Sometimes, of course, *for
these reasons or in order to attract attention,* he
senses that he must speak out and express himself,
but since he drifts with the tide of events, by the
time he makes his move it's too late *and he's left
behind. Moreover, it teaches him not to make waves
again in the future.*

        The Weststruck man is religiously indifferent.
He doesn't believe in anything, but neither does he
disbelieve anything. He's mixed up. He's an oppor-
tunist. Everything's all the same to him. He thinks
of himself first, and once his donkey gets across the
bridge he doesn't care if the bridge is there or not.
He has no faith, no principles, no platform, no
belief in God or humanity. He's indifferent to social progress and even to *religion and* irreligion.
He's not even irreligious. He's just indifferent.

        He does go to the mosque sometimes, of course,
just as he goes to /party meetings,/ *the club,* or the
cinema, but he's just a spectator everywhere, like
someone watching a football game. He's always on the
sidelines. You'll never see him in the ring. He

never gets personally involved, not even so far as to
shed a tear when a friend dies, to stop and reflect
at a shrine, or to think about anything when he's
alone. He's totally unaccustomed to being alone. He
avoids it. Since he's afraid of himself, he goes
everywhere. He votes, of course, *if there is an
election, and especially* if it's fashionable, but for
the *person,* /party or power/ that seems most likely
to serve his interests. You'll never hear a cry,
complaint, or an "if," "and," or "but" out of him.
He explains everything away in florid, self-assured
language, setting himself up as an optimist.

He's a Weststruck man of leisure. He believes
in living for today, but not in any philosophical
sense. If his automobile is in good shape, and he's
well groomed and dressed, nothing else matters. If
Sa'di was prevented from traveling in the old days
because of "problems with his family, clothing, and
food," this man, engrossed with filling his own
stomach, worries about no one else. He doesn't let
himself worry. He shrugs everything off easily.
Since he's planned his own life and does everything
according to plan, and since every action has an
equal and opposite reaction, he has nothing to do
with other people, *to say nothing of their aches and
pains.*

A Weststruck man /usually/ has no specialty.
He's a jack-of-all-trades and master of none. Since
he has studied, read books, and gone to school,
however, he knows how to make an impression on any
group with high-sounding talk. He may even have had
a specialty at one time, but he learned later that in
these provinces it isn't possible to bribe the right
people using just one skill, and he was forced to
take up other activities.

He's acquired the fussy effeminacy of the old
woman in the family who knows a little bit about everything as a result of her long life and years of
experience. The Weststruck man knows a little bit
about everything too, and certainly about his own
<u>Gharbzadegi</u>, the fashion of the day, useful for
television stations, /useful for radio stations, useful for classes and lessons,/ useful for
/joint/ educational commissions and planning seminars, useful for high-circulation newspapers, *and
even for speeches at the club.*

A Weststruck man has no personality--he isn't

genuine. Neither he himself, nor his home, nor what
he has to say gives off any kind of odor. He's all
things to all people. Not that he's cosmopolitan or
a world-state advocate. Never. He doesn't belong
anywhere. Not that he belongs everywhere. He's a
combination of a person without personality and a
person without character. Because he's insecure he's
dissimulative. He doesn't trust the person he's
talking to even when he's doing his best to show
goodwill and friendliness. Since skepticism is
everywhere among us, he never opens his heart. The
only characteristic that can be understood and seen
in him is fear. If people's personalities are
sacrificed to specialization in the West, a
Weststruck man has no personality and no specialty.
He has only fear. Fear of tomorrow, fear of losing
his job, fear of being a nobody, fear of the dis-
closure that that bladder weighing down his head
serving as his brain is empty.[5]

The Weststruck man is prissy.[6] He takes very
good care of himself. He's always fussing with his
personal wardrobe and grooming. *He even plucks the
hair under his eyebrows sometimes.* His shoes, his
clothing, /his vehicle,/ and his house, are extremely
important to him. He always looks as if he just came
out of the box, or out of some European fashion
house. He changes the model of his car every year.
His house, which once had a basement, an indoor pond,
a porch, a canopy, a balcony, *and a vestibule*, now
takes on a new imitative shape every day. One day it
resembles a villa by the sea, with huge picture windows and fluorescent lights.[7] One day it looks like
a cabaret, sparkling, shiny, and full of bar stools.
Another day all the walls are the same background
color, with every surface covered by bunches of
multicolored triangles. Every corner of the house,
no matter what, is full of Western industrial
products. One corner has a hi-fi, another a television, another a /player/ piano for his pampered
daughter, another stereo speakers. The kitchen and
every other nook and cranny are also full of gas ranges, automatic washing machines, and other things of
this nature. The Weststruck man is the most loyal
consumer of Western industrial products. If he ever
got up in the morning and found that all the barber
shops, tailors, and shoeshine and repair shops had
closed, the shock of it would strike him down, feet
pointed to Mecca.[8] Of course, he doesn't know which
direction that is.

The availability of all these activities and
products I've listed is more necessary to him than
any school, mosque, hospital, or factory. It's because of him that we have such artificial, alien architecture, and such incongruous city design.' It's
because of him that the streets and crossroads of the
cities are lit up like a penny arcade with lurid
fluorescent and neon lights. It's because of him
that a way-to-the-stomach gourmet cookbook called The
Way to the Heart[10] was printed, full of recipes for
dishes requiring cream and meat, foods that absolutely cannot be had in our hot, dry climate, dishes that
were devised merely *as an excuse* to utilize European
gas ranges.

It's because of him that they destroy the arches
in the bazaars.[11] It's because of him that they
destroyed the Takiyeh-ye Dowlat. ' It's because of
him that the senate building is such a monstrosity.
We also have this man to thank if the soldiers wear
so much glitter their uniforms look like variety
store displays.

A Weststruck man is in awe of the West. He
wants nothing to do with what happens in this little
world of our own--a corner in the East. If he happens to be a politician, he knows about the subtlest
leanings to the right or the left in the British
Labor Party, and he knows the American senators better than he knows the government ministries in his
own country. He knows the names and reputations of
Time and News Chronicle commentators better than he
knows his distant cousin in /Khorasan/ [or] *Bandar
Abbas*, and he gives more credence to what they say
than to the words of a divine prophet. *And why? Because all these people have more effect on what happens in his country than any politician, analyst, or
domestic representative.* If his field is literature
and rhetoric, he is only interested in knowing who
won the Nobel prize for literature this year, who got
the Goncourt prize,[12] who got the Pulitzer prize, /or
what some European magazine wrote about Lolita./ *And
if he's a researcher, he sits on his hands and ig-
nores all the issues that merit his attention in this
country. He concerns himself only with what such-
and-such an orientalist wrote and said about the issues that deserve his research.* If, however, he's
one of the common people, and a follower of the slick
weekly picture magazines, well, we've all seen what a
smart fellow he is.

In any event, if there was once a time when a
spoken verse from the Qur'an or a prophetic tradition
in Arabic would command silence from everyone and
make every critic sit still, now a line quoted from
some Westerner will close every mouth on any occasion.

The situation has gotten so shameful in this
regard that Western forecasters, fortune-tellers, and
astrologers have suddenly put the whole world in a
state of turmoil and fear. Divine inspiration now
comes from Western books instead of holy books, or
else the mouths of UPI, Reuters, and AP reporters.
These giant news companies, processors of fake news
and real news! It's true that knowledge of scientific methods, the technique and methods of machine
construction and the West's philosophical principles
can only be found in European and Western books, but
a Weststruck man, who has nothing to do with the
principles of Western philosophy--when he wants to
know something about the East--consults Western sources. This is how, in Weststruck countries, the subject of orientalism (which is, in all probability, a
parasite that has grown on the rotting roots of
colonialism) has come to prevail over the minds and
ideas of the people.

A Weststruck man, instead of using Western sources just to find the principles of Western civilization, does so only to find what is not Western. In
the philosophy of Islam, for example, the Jhoki customs of the Indians, the study of how superstition
spread in Indonesia, the spirit of nationalism among
the Arabs, or any other Eastern subject, he considers
Western writings the only good sources. The
Weststruck man even describes, *understands*, and
/explains/ himself in the language of orientalists!
/He solemnly lets it be known that he participated in
some orientalist congress or that his and his
father's name and that of his country's poet were
listed by some orientalist on this or that page of an
orientalist encyclopedia./ *He has placed himself, an*
imagined thing, under the orientalist's microscope,
and he depends on what the orientalist sees, not on
what he is, feels, and experiences. This is the
ugliest manifestation of <u>Gharbzadegi</u>.[14] Consider
yourself nothing, abandon all confidence in yourself,
and in your own eyes, ears, and vision. Turn over
all your intellectual capacity to every incompetent
writer who's said or written something as an orientalist. I certainly don't know when this orientalism

became a science. If we say some Westerner is a
specialist in Eastern languages, dialects, or music,
I agree with that, or if we say he's an
anthropologist or a sociologist, again I agree to a
certain extent. But what does orientalism mean, in
general? *Is it knowledge of all the secrets of the
Eastern world? Are we living in the time of Aristotle?* I say it's a parasite growing on the roots of
colonialism. *What's funny is that this orientalist
who depends on UNESCO has his organizations too, and
his congress every two to four years, and member-
ships, and coming and going, and such a lot of carrying on....* /Think of your own examples. It's better
that I not mention any names./

   The unfortunate thing here is that our contemporary leaders--especially those who are involved in
both politics and literature (and unfortunately this
is itself another characteristic of politics and
political leadership in Weststruck countries, *where
most of the politicians are men of letters, bearded
and mustachioed litterateurs, and the process has exactly reversed itself, meaning that any politician in
the leadership has to write a book too*)--are under
the influence of these Western orientalists. They
were the student of some orientalist professor at one
time, who came here himself, who had come *secretly or
openly* into the service of his country's foreign ministry by learning an Eastern language, being without
any specialty in his own Western country, and
unskilled at any art, profession, specialization, or
technique. He was exported to this part of the world
right along with Western machine manufacturing, *or as
a reconnaissance scout for it, along with a few technicians, so that while selling Western manufactures
he could kill some time learning poetry and cheering
the heart of his loyal buyer, who would say "Yes,
did you see, did you hear? So-and-so was speaking
Farsi so well!"* This is how we have orientalists,
with their books, research, excavations, poetry
studies and musicology. In the middle of this hot
market for machines, the Western orientalist comes
and writes a biography of Mulla Sadra[1] for us, or
gives an opinion concerning our belief *or unbelief* in
the Imam of the Age, *or does research on the merits
of Shaykh Pashm od-Din Keshkuli.*[1] Not only do all
Weststruck individuals everywhere cite their
opinions, but we've heard them cite Carlisle, Gustave
Le Bon, de Gobineau, and Edward Browne many times on
the pulpits and in the mosques as well (which are
supposedly the last line of defense against the West

and <u>Gharbzadegi</u>) as the ultimate supporting documents
for the reliability of some person, act, or religious
path

Of course we're very right to say that since the
Western man, *with all his university and research
facilities and libraries crammed to the gills*, uses
the scientific method even in the study of Eastern
language, religion, and literature, *he has better op-
portunities and a broader perspective. It's no wonder
then that his words and opinions are better sources
than those of the Easterners themselves, who have
neither the scientific method nor those research
facilities. And perhaps Eastern sources must also be
mainly sought in the West because the museums,
libraries, and universities on that end of the world
are full of plundered relics, artifacts, and
libraries from this end of the world. A Western
researcher inevitably has more resources available on
Eastern issues.* Perhaps another reason these sciences are more likely to be found in the West is that
the Easterner himself has not yet entered into these
worlds, being still caught up in a day-to-day
struggle to feed and clothe himself, and not having
yet found the time to discuss divinity and mortality.
And a thousand other 'perhapses'. For me, all these
'perhapses' are certainties. What would he say,
however, in a case where the Westerner and the
Easterner had each given opinions, and each arrived
at a different conclusion by the same method? Don't
you think, in such a situation, that in the eyes of
our Weststruck man the Western opinion would still
have priority over the Eastern one? I've experienced
this /misfortune/ personally a number of times.

And as a final point--a Weststruck individual in
this province knows absolutely nothing about the
petroleum issue. *He has nothing to say about it, because his interests here and in the hereafter are not
there. And even though he sometimes makes his living
solely through this means, he never gets a whiff of
the actual oil. No comment, no talk, no reference,
and no "buts"! Never. The surrender to oil is un-
conditional. And if he does get involved with it, he
works in the petroleum service industries or as a
broker. He even writes magazines for them (see
<u>Kavosh</u> magazine) and makes films (see <u>Mowj ow Marjan
ow Khara</u>) [Waves, coral, and granite], but ignoring
the facts. A Weststruck person is not a dreamer, not
an idealist. He's dealing with reality, and reality
in this province requires the transfer of oil without
disruption.*

NOTES

[1]The cultural equivalent of a 'paper tiger'.
(tr)

[2]*I've been criticized for ignoring the people's
political struggles in this booklet, from the Constitutional Revolution until today. I haven't ignored these struggles. I've passed over them in
silence, because if the leaders of all these struggles had been right (with all their losses to imprisonment, murder, and exile,) our condition would
be better than this. Of course, the people aren't to
blame for all these defeats. It's the misguided
leadership of these struggles that has brought on
such consequences.* (A)

[3]Mount Uhud is located in Saudi Arabia in the
vicinity of Mecca. (tr)

[4]*See Sukhan magazine, Khordad 1340 [May 22-June
21, 1961].* (A)

[5]*For affirmation of these points see Iran az
Yad Naborim [Let's not forget Iran], by my dear
friend Mohammad 'Ali Islami Nudushan, Entesharat-e
Majalleh-ye Yaghma, Esfand 1340 [Feb 20-Mar 20,
1962].* (A)

[6]*Concerning this prissyness or dandyism see
this same Taskhir-e Tamadon-e Farangi [The subjugation of European culture] by Seyed Fakhrod-Din Shadman, (Tehran: 1326) [1947 or 48], to which I referred
earlier.* (A)

[7]*Note these few lines I've taken from a large
color advertisement in the newspaper Ettela'at (Or-
debehesht 19, 1342) [May 9, 1963], p. 12, about some
newly-built suburban development on the outskirts of
Tehran, and its virtues: "The special mechanisms and
astonishing features of this little city have
definitely brought a corner of European or American
architectural style into our country. The modern
villas of this summer resort town will captivate
aficionados of Western civilization (sic) and those
who have been educated there so that they will always
feel that they are living in Europe or America...."*

Does it get more expressive than this?   (A)

    ⁹Muslim burial position. (tr)

    ⁸We had gone to buy a house for a friend.
There was a house in Darus that had been copied exactly from the churches [Charles Edouard Jeanneret
Le] Corbusier had built in a modern style, known by
the name Notre-Dame du Hout. The only thing it
didn't have was the tower, but it had the same nooks,
corners, ceilings, and so on.... (A)

    ¹⁰A very flashy, slick, expensive book titled
Rah-e Del [The way to the heart], written or translated by Mrs. Yusufi, printed by Ebn-e Sina. (A)

    ¹¹See "Chand Kalimeh ba Mashateha" [A few words
with some bride-dressers] by this writer in the
magazine Andisheh va Honar [Thought and art], Aban
1337 [Oct 23-Nov 21, 1958]. On the same subject is
the article "Karavansera-ye Safavi Esfahanra Cheguneh
Kharab Kardand?"[How did they destroy the Safavid
caravanserais in Esfahan?] by Abol Hoseyn Sepanta in
the Farvardin 1342 [Mar 21-Ap 20, 1963] issue of the
magazine Armaghan.

    Aside from these things my dear friend Taqi
Fadakar relates from his childhood memories that he
witnessed how, early in Reza Shah's reign, they
destroyed the municipal minaret, which was at the
head of the road to Yazd alongside the Zayandeh
River, in order to build a military barracks with its
bricks at the ruins at Farrokhabad Garden in Esfahan.
The minaret had two stairwells, and such intricate
detail and historical and architectural importance.
And on whose orders was this done? The orders of the
Swedish General [sic] Gleerup, who was military chief
of staff or some such thing in Esfahan. He said they
propped the minaret up on one side and gutted the
base on the same side. Then they wrapped blankets
around the support beams, soaked them in oil, and set
it afire. When the beams burned the minaret fell
over on that side. And that was it! (A) [Trans-
lators' note: Gleerup, a Colonel, was commander of
the Esfahan Gendarmerie.]

    ¹²The result of this very 'whoever came built a
new building', the initiative of people like Engineer
Forughi. And what's more it was done to build the
Bazaar branch of the Bank-e Melli, not on the same
spot, but way over to one side. (A)

¹³An annual French literary prize awarded by the Academie Goncourt, founded by Edmond de Goncourt (1822-1896). (tr)

¹⁴*For the most recent example of this see the article "Dar Mahzar-e 'Aref-e Irani"* [In the presence of an Iranian Sufi] *by Jan Rypka in the first through the third issues of the magazine <u>Rahnama-ye Ketab</u>* [Book Guide], *Farvardin to Khordad, 1342* [Mar 21¬Jun 21, 1963]. *It's an article full of the praises of Shaykh Shams ol-Orafa and his mystical power, and so on... And remember that this gentleman Jan Rypka came to Iran as a translator along with the Czechoslovakian (Skoda) specialists during the twenty-year era and then wrote a history of literature for us!* (A) [Translators' note: The 'twenty-year era' was the period of the reign of Reza Shah, from 1921 to 1941. 'Skoda' is the name of an automobile manufactured in Czechoslovakia.]

¹⁵Mulla Sadra, Muhammad ibn Ibrahim, d. 1641, Sufi and Islamic theologian. (tr)

¹⁶The author has invented this name as a joke at the expense of the Sufis and the Westerners who study them. 'Pashm od-Din' means 'the wool of religion', a reference to the beard usually worn by the Sufis. 'Keshkuli' means 'beggar's bowl-bearing'. (tr)

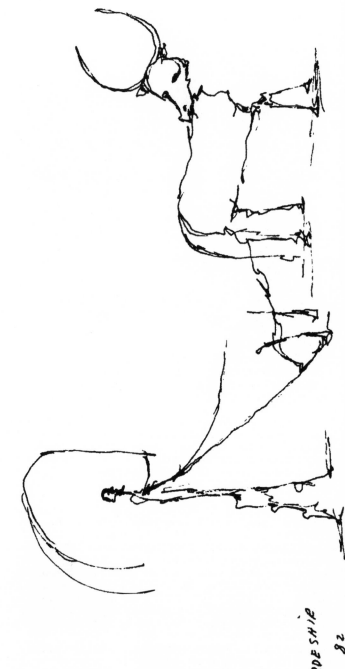

ARDESHIR
82

8

A SOCIETY IN DISORDER

What characteristics does a society led by these leaders--I mean our Weststruck society--have? Economically and socially we saw how our society is entangled with incongruous institutions.

It's a mixture of a pastoral economy and a village economy with the manners of a newly formed urbanity, ruled by big foreign economic interests like a trust or a cartel. *We're a living museum of old and new social institutions.* /We have all of this at once./

At least 1.5 million of the people in this country are still nomads. This is an official statistic, which means it's a doctored statistic. If you ask the Ministry of Defense or the Royal Tribal Administration Office, they say. the tribes number something more than three million people,[1] people who are unattached to the land and who destroy everything civilized in their path. They thrive on sheep herding. Ninety-five percent of them are living embodiments of poverty, adversity, and homelessness. They wander the year around in search of the most fundamental requirement of life--water. They're vagrants, *going from summer to winter quarters and back again.* Yet the initiative for all our domestic and foreign political conflagration is in the hands

of their leaders, who are nominally border guardians
loyal to the shah. Instead of being loyal, however,
they practice extortion to excess, and in reality
they bring insecurity with them wherever they go,
and *destruction* and fear.

Their leaders participate in official ceremonies
and send congratulatory telegrams on every occasion,
but they're a constant threat to anyone who con-
templates building anything within their tribal
domain. The Khan of Basht still extracts so many
thousand tumans tribute every year from the powerful
oil company [The National Iranian Oil Company]. The
Khan of Hayat Davudi pressured the government to
transfer Khark Island to the oil consortium for his
own purposes. The Khan of Qashqa'i² set himself up
in Switzerland and now awaits an opportune moment to
return and seize power. (*And we saw on Nowruz of
1341*) [Mar 21 1962] *how the government's supporters
laid waste to his mansion and livelihood in
Firuzabad.*³ If the Bakhtiaris are quiet now it's
because ever since the Constitutional Revolution
they've found favor in high places, as well as seats
in the Senate, the *directorship* of the *Security* Organization,⁴ and so on.

In this country, to get anything done it is
first necessary to settle the tribes, but not, of
course, the way we've been doing it. Not by force
and by trampling on them, but by a precise, logical,
and well-considered method; by designating land and
water for each person; by preparing new agricultural
means for each group; by buying their surplus
animals; by persuading the people themselves in each
tribe to participate in the building of their future
homes; and by establishing centers for health, education, and mechanical repair for every newly established village. /Don't ask me to prescribe a
remedy for every pain. It's enough to know˙ the way
to the cure./ In any case, as long as tribal tent
posts are not converted to village houses, and tribal
men and women remain unfamiliar with agriculture and
their children don't sit down to study under the roof
of a school, any measure to improve matters in this
country is either a lie, demagoguery, or a childish
pretense. *And then in a situation like this, our
governmental policy concerning the tribes is to
leave them to fend for themselves until they waste
away with poverty and chronic disease, trembling in
the face of continual drought conditions, and until
the last breath of life has gone out of them, and*

not even a trace remains!

We've also seen that *sixty or* seventy percent oſ
our zealous population lives in villages, the condition of which I've described earlier in this book,
and also in Orazan and Tat Neshinha-ye Boluk-e Zah-
ra.⁵   The rest live in cities. While the villages
thin out day-by-day, newly erected cities are booming
and growing day-by-day, exactly like cancerous
tumors! Cities spring up on every side of the desert
like mushrooms, with no prior planning for their
water, power, streets, telephones, or sewage. Are
they comparable to anything, other than cancer? We
pluck people out of the villages and add them to the
cities, cities that differ in no way from the villages except that there's work to be found in them,
albeit of a temporary and seasonal nature. Yet
there's no work at all in the villages.

In the last ten years they've made a bad situation worse by dabbling in pseudochange. In reality,
this merely adds to the class of the petty landlords.
If this petty landlord class had been bolstered two-
hundred years ago, *at least* now we'd have a decent
constitution, but now the name of the game is
cooperatives. It's too late to divide up property
into small tracts. Property division of this kind
now will pose a formidable obstacle for the new
mechanized agriculture. Machines and petty landowners don't go together, because petty landowners
can't obtain these new tools, and they aren't
designed for their needs anyway. With our in-
dividualistic spirit and the tendency in each of us
to go his own way, it's unrealistic to believe that
the majority of the people in a village would get
together on their own and pool their resources to
bring a machine into the village. *I'll curtail my
remarks concerning this matter and defer to my friend
Hoseyn Malek, who has propounded a very detailed plan
on the matter of agriculture in various issues of the
magazine 'Elm va Zendigi and presented it for publié
consideration.*⁶

/In a country like ours any social or economic
activity must be predetermined. Nothing can be left
to fate or the future. As things are now, every village must be preserved just as it is, but it must be
managed so as to prevent the government and landlords
from taking out salaries and shares for themselves.
These shares and salaries must be diverted to the
development of roads, schools, health care, water,

power, and machinery in the village. Maybe a common
fund for these monies could be established in each
village for use in the village, in order to gradually
instill the idea of a cooperative and its advantages
in the minds of the village people. After they
realize it isn't a trick and begin to believe in it,
perhaps they will take on the remainder of the task
of socializing the land and the agricultural activity
on their own. It is through this type of process
that this exodus from the land can be stopped. When
a person leaves his village, someone must ask why
he's leaving, where he's going, and whether there's a
place for him to live in the city, and a way must be
sought to find work and living accommodations for him
in the village itself./

In any event, until they stop this mischievous
village conscription, and as long as the temptation
of the cities exists and the terror of passing tribes
remains, the villages will never flourish. As long
as roads don't reach the villages, electricity
doesn't light village homes, and there are no repair
shops for agricultural equipment, each one serving
thirty or forty villages, there will be no mechanized
agriculture. As long as petty landlords still
predominate, and as long as a mechanic's class isn't
established near every school, machines will be alien
to the villages, and if they do come to a village,
they will be no more than a source of destruction,
excitement, and confusion.

As for the cities--these cancerous organs--they
grow and expand day by day into grotesqueness and
superficiality. Every day they demand more Western
industrial products. Day by day they become more totally decadent, rootless, and *ugly*. Every one of
them is just a crossroads with a statue [of the shah]
ordered up by the government. At the center of the
square, the bazaar's arches have collapsed, and the
neighborhoods are far removed from one another,
without water, power, telephones, social services,
meeting places, or libraries. The mosques are
ruined. The <u>hosseiniyyehs</u> are crumbling and collaps-
ing, and the <u>takiyehs</u> have now lost their meaning.'
There are no parties, no clubs, no public parks or
recreation facilities. They have nothing better to
offer than one or two cinemas, none of them any more
than a means of arousing the people sexually, places
to kill time or indulge in pointless amusement. Our
cinemas neither teach us nor help change our thinking. It may be stated with assurance that, in this

part of the world, every theater is simply a piggy
bank ' where every city resident drops two or three
tumans a week in order to make millionaires of the
principal Metro Goldwyn Mayer stockholders.'

The molders of our urban public opinion are
either these movies, government radio, or popular
photo magazines. All of these media strive to encourage conformity, to make everyone everywhere part
of the same piece of cloth. The houses are all
alike, clothing is all the same, as are luggage,
plastic tableware, grooming styles, and worst of all,
modes of thought. This is the most prominent threat
to our newly formed urbanity.

If conformity of thinking and behavior is
dangerous enough in an advanced society to put man at
the service of machines, for us, who are only consumers of machines, it's doubly dangerous. It
enslaves us to machines with twice the force. A
Westerner in the service of machines at least knows
of democracy, because political parties are a sequel
to machines. We don't have political parties,
however, /because we don't manufacture machines/--
with our schools that reduce the number of religious
societies every day, and our involvement with a form
of government that's been around since time
immemorial--and if we're going to become slaves to
machines on top of all that, woe be unto us from then
on! We'll lose everything, principal and interest,
both outwardly and inwardly.

In such a society, the large opinion-molding institutions must not be controlled by one or two companies (such as television--this isn't America!) nor
under government control (such as the radio--this
isn't a country behind the iron curtain!). /Such organizations, in an underdeveloped country, must be
led by the government only, a government that cares
about the people in this age of change, that helps
them, guides them, and seeks to find solutions and
procedures./' In a developing country such as ours
such facilities must be controlled by society for
society's benefit, and be administered by an elected
council of writers and intellectuals with no personal
material or propagandizing objectives.

It's been fashionable for some time to talk of
large landowners, of the threat of large, immovable
estates, ignoring the fact that these days the large
landed estates are no longer profitable. We can see

that the shah and others are now talking about dividing up land holdings. They *mistakenly*[10] hold this up
as the solution to all problems.

The dangerous things these days are the big
moveable estates, money, stocks, bank credit, capital
deposited in foreign banks, powerful individuals who
have their fingers in industry, the power of big
stockholders and domestic *and foreign cartels* and
trusts, and especially those who, if I may say so,
manage the educational industries, /and publish
newspapers and books/. *It is necessary to be thinking
about these things and make plans to nationalize or
'socialize' them.*

Politically, we live with a self-interested and
careless government, notwithstanding its feeble attempts to exude the manifestations of freedom, which
are just window dressing for the assembly. It's
self-interested because there's no refuge from it, no
hope, no freedom, and no rights. It's careless because despite all this there's still room to breathe
and let off steam quietly by screaming into a well.[11]
One may see this, because the ordinary man in the
street--though he be dressed in the armed uniform of
a government *servant* or censor--is still, deep in his
heart, the same heedless 'this too will pass'
unprejudiced fellow, who has not yet become a dry,
rigid mechanical nut or bolt in the hands of institutions because of machines. And rue the day when we
also lose this only and final vestige of backwardness
and primitivity.

The army, in any event, prevails in the end over
everything, is the final arbiter of every situation
and first in line for privileges in this country!
Officially and publicly thirty percent and unoffi-
cially around fifty-four percent of this country's
whole budget is spent on maintaining the combined
forces of the military, in addition to all the
foreign handouts that promote only the military's
welfare, over and above the public welfare.[12] Never
mind that legislation in this country was as ineffec-
tive in the past as it is now, that the judicial and
executive powers aggressively interfere with one
another, and that administrative organizations still
move as slowly as they did in the days when couriers
rode mules. All these things are symptoms. The
basic problem is that this weak body cannot support
such a huge, pretentious, sickly head!

When asked to explain why we have all these armies, they say they're for the purpose of defending
our borders and our unified nation, but beneath the
surface....? We've seen how borders are so easily
crossed by companies, and we've seen how our unified
nation gets dissipated from within. *Which invasion
is it that we have to confront for defense?*

Neither on the twentieth of Shahrivar nor on the
twenty-eighth of Mordad were all these soldiers and
weapons of any use to us![13] The whole point of all
the military institutions that fill this country from
top to bottom is to keep 150 thousand (*of course this
is an official figure*) of the nation's finest youths
armed to the teeth--irrespective of the fact that
things are never as they should be here in this hot
market for change with its frenzied, relentless
construction--and to nurture and train them to
preserve the strength and continuity of a private
government that relies on their power. It is inad-
visable that all these workers' hands be put to tasks
every year in the name of military service that con-
tribute absolutely nothing to national capital formation.

In times like these we must not, in the name of
conscription, empty the villages of their vital manpower and bring these people to /live as parasites
feeding on others in/ military barracks, /depriving
the people of bread and/ learning to wage war against
some unspecified future enemy. We cannot sit idly by
while every year at least three-hundred thousand
strong men are made to bear arms and train at activities which have done nothing for us on any occasion since the seige of Herat.[14] Moreover, this is
happening at a time when mutual defense is a priority
program even for advanced industrial governments, /at
a time when local resistance failed in Azarbaijan,
Korea, Vietnam, and Algeria,/ in a period when the
fate of governments and world political boundaries
are decided /only by the politicians of governments
that build machines, and/ not on the battlefield but
at the conference table. *In this day and age, it's a
joke anymore to talk of obtaining new donated artillery. To go parading with tanks and artillery and
to train paratroopers and commandos only serve to
suppress the young peoples' demonstrations at the
university or to quell the rioting of theology students at Fayziyeh Madraseh,*[15] *and there's no need for
so many weapons and men to quell such minor uprisings.*

Let's take an impartial look at Japan and Germany, who were only able to summon the strength to
rebuild their totally destroyed economies after World
War II because of compulsory disarmament, and who
have done this so well that now, after fewer than
twenty years, their competitive threat to the conquering nations is causing alarm in marketplaces the
world over. Do you think that if these two governments had decided to waste most of their economic
power and human resources on armaments, as they did
before the war, they would have been as successful as
they are today in the matters of political and
economic reconstruction? In this day and age, when
the ultimate cure for Algeria after eight years of
war and bloodshed was to abandon Saharan oil and
declare independence, what is the use of soldiers
and weapons? *Other than to allow brothers to kill
each other?* France, with all its greatness, its
weapons, paratroopers, *and commandos,* couldn't defeat
ten million Algerians. Who are we going to face with
our 150 thousand soldiers? It is in our interest to
forget the army and be satisfied with the police and
the gendarmerie *as security forces.* If we cannot
boldly pursue this plan, definitely and assuredly we
must convert all army barracks to centers of learning
for technologies and professions that will rebuild
the villages, and make them places for acquainting
today's soldiers--the villagers of the future--with
the skills, techniques, *and general and specialized
knowledge* necessary to every village community. [18]

Another striking point in the domain of politics
is our /childish/ affectation of Western democracy.
That is, we pretend to be a democracy. It has nothing to do with actual Western democracy /and it cannot have, but our governments affect it/. *Its conditions and requirements--freedom of speech, freedom to
express ideas, freedom to utilize the communications
media (which are a government monopoly), freedom to
publish ideas in opposition to the authorities in
power--none of these things exist--*but our government
puts on a democratic facade, in order to silence this
or that political opponent /at home/ or abroad, *from
whom it would like to obtain financial credit.* We've
seen that the foundation of Western democracy is
political parties, that political parties are functions of advanced economic development, and that when
they precede it they turn into political factions, of
which we have many. These party-like groupings of
ours, if they aren't special interest groups organized to acquire wealth and prestige or the result

of a royal decree ordering their formation--*and
short-lived--will* certainly be no more than
factions--factions that, /lacking a free hand in
political activities and struggles/ *(there are no
clubs, the press isn't free, and party and street
gatherings aren't allowed)* have contented themselves
with operating secretly and being self-styled martyrs. These factions, whether religious or political
in color, are no more than seeds of resistance that
may someday be useful. Because they're isolated from
the people and don't have their hands in the fire,
the lines of communication between them and the
people are blocked and their cries are not
heartfelt. Thus the most these factions can do is be
the basis of a likely movement for some foreign
policy in need of a local, national base of operations.

Most of the coups d'etat and sudden rotations of
government in this corner of the East take place in
the name of these very factions, if not at the hands
of those groupings. But they're really acting on be-
half of foreign political interests. In any case,
what is indisputable is that we cannot claim to be a
Western democracy in a situation like this. It is
neither possible nor in our interests for us to do
this. Putting on a Western democratic facade is itself another symptom of <u>Gharbzadegi</u>.[17]

*If there was a time when landowners trucked
voters by force from the village to the ballot box,
on the sixth of Bahman [Jan 26, 1963] and at the
elections, we've seen since that they put the
municipal ballot boxes right in the doorways of the
ministries and administration buildings and distributed circulars saying that salaries for the following month would be paid upon presentation of an
election receipt! It was a perfect example of the
story about bringing the load to the donkey. And
with all this, such pretensions about free elections
and the huge voter turnout!*

*We'll only be able to discuss democracy in this
country--that is, the opinion and will of the people
can only be manifested when:*

*A - The powerful local leaders, the big lan-
downers, and the remnants of the feudal system--who
are an obstacle to free balloting for the people--
have been deprived of their power and influence,*

B - The publishing and broadcast media are not monopolized by the current governments, but are also their opponents,

C - Political parties, not in the guise of despicable political groupings, have truly gained the power to operate and an extensive realm in which to do so,

D - Interference by security forces and (the Security Organization [SAVAK]) has been unequivocally stopped.

There was a time when everyone was screaming and protesting the absence of freedom, because the one who would end up getting the people's vote--aside from the <u>kedkhoda</u> [village chief], the gendarmerie, the governing power, the landowners, and the district chiefs--was whoever compensated the voters for time away from work so they could spend half a day taking them to the ballot box and back. Now, however, when the Security Organization [SAVAK] stuffs the ballot box and makes up the ballot as well, what can be said? Now there's not even any use in screaming about it. Whenever the country's intellectuals have been defeated the Security Organization has been the winner. The end of every thread [the intellectuals] have spun has ended up in the hands of this upstart institution, which so controls things with terror, threats, corruption, imprisonment, and exile that nothing ever happens and the two assemblies will convene right on time without a hitch. And why have things turned out this way, anyway? Because the people have no idea of the concept of democracy--and if they have had such ideas they must have been unimpressed by these liberationist claims to have now so silently and peacefully surrendered their fate to intellectual surrogates.

In any case, until the concept of democracy has penetrated society deeply with extended education and training and until the people have become acquainted--in a true and accurate sense--with the political party system, talk of democracy in this country is fit only for those politicians in the Majlis whose donkeys have already gotten over the bridge and who need the nation's vote to justify their positions.

NOTES

[1]"*According to the (November) 1962 census, Iran's tribes make up fifteen percent of the population. Of the remainder, twenty-five percent live in cities and sixty percent live in villages. Because of some historical factors, feudalism and the tribal system evolved together in Iran. The only power capable of holding its own in the feudal system was the tribal system. It's no accident that all the ruling dynasties which came to power in Iran arose from the tribes. Even in the time of the Constitutional Revolution and its disturbances, the tribal khans (Bakhtiari) and the big landowners (Sipahsalar Tonkaboni and others) participated officially.*" From page 419 of the Echo of Iran Almanac for the year 1963, published in Tehran in English. See Iran Almanac-1963, Pub. by Echo of Iran. (A)

[2]The three aforementioned 'khans' (chieftains) are all tribal leaders. (tr)

[3]The 1962 date given here in the Farsi text is probably a misprint. The author is most likely referring to a series of government reprisals directed at the Qashqa'i tribes in March 1963 intended to suppress their attempts to obstruct the government's land-reform program that had just gotten under way. (tr)

[4]A reference to General Timur Bakhtiyar, former chief of the Sazman-i Ettela'at va Amniyyat-e Keshvar (The National Intelligence and Security Organization, better known as SAVAK). See Cottam, op. cit., pp. 63, 302. (tr)

[5]/Both these booklets are published by Entesharat-e Danesh, Sa'di, Tehran./ (A)

[6]Concerning this see 'Elm va Zendigi's issues for 1338 [Mar 21, 1959-Mar 20, 1960], volumes 4, 5, and 6 (which are devoted exclusively to land reform) and finally in volume 10, Aban 1339 [Oct 23-Nov, 21 1960], of the same magazine. All of these things were written and said before the current redivision of property began. (A)

7Hosseiniyyehs are places where the martyrdom of Imam Hossein is mourned, or in which passion plays, reenactments of the imam's martyrdom, are sometimes performed. A takiyeh is a religious theater where passion plays are presented. (tr)

8"Every month the people of Tehran spend 23 million tumans at the movies. The theater owners make an 800 percent profit on every film." This was the heading of an article reprinted by the magazine Khwandaniha (no. 6, 30 Mordad, 1341 [August 21, 1962] from another publication, Rowshanfekr. (A)

9/I predicted in "Belbeshu-ye Ketabha-ye Darsi" [The confusion in textbooks] that the first monopolies in our country after oil would be the press, and this is becoming a reality. Franklin [publishers] can no longer tolerate a rival press organization. Sokhan cannot tolerate another magazine, and the government no longer accepts new publications./ (A)

10The earlier edition uses the term bedorugh (deceitfully) here. (tr)

11There is an Iranian folk tale about a barber who noticed that the infant Alexander the Great had a horn on his head while he was giving him a haircut. The barber was sworn to secrecy on this, but the burden of such a secret was unbearable for him. He would vent his frustration from time to time by going to the mouth of a water well and screaming "Alexander has a horn" down into it. Years later a musician who happened to pass by the well cut a branch of bamboo that was growing out its side and fashioned a flute from it. He then proceeded to Alexander's court to play. As soon as he blew into the instrument the sound came out, "Alexander has a horn." The story suggests that ways may be found to give effective expression to frustration without inviting unpleasant repercussions. (tr)

12Even the major newspapers discuss the power of the military these days (1340). See the two articles "Arzyabi-ye Naqsh-e Artesh" [Evaluating the army's role] by Daryush Homayun in no. 10820 (19 Khordad, 1341/June 9, 1962) and no. 10841 (16 Tir, 1341/July 7, 1962) of the semiofficial newspaper Ettela'at, and this Daryush Homayun is one of Ettela'at's best writers. Several lines from the first article: "The army of Iran is so vast in relation to the resources and possibilities of the country that economic and social growth must stand aside for it. Defense considerations must be provided for, but the overall role of the army is domestic... (and at the end of the same article) ...in a country like Iran the manpower and facilities in the armed forces are not to be overlooked in the matter of building the nation." Here are several lines from the second article: "The army of Iran, with close to 150,000 armed men, a huge share of the budget and national income and tens of thousands of men who enter and leave its ranks every year, is not a separate social organization that may be left responsible only for protecting independence and security. Have they not yet understood in our country that without reliance on international defense systems our military establishment has no capacity to engage anything?" (A) [Translators' note: The image of Daryush Homayun among Iranians is not that of critic of the imperial establishment, despite the critical tone in these quotes. He is credited with authorship of an infamous article planted by the shah's government under a pseudonym in the newspapers Ettela'at and Ayandegan on January 7, 1978, entitled "Iran va Este'margaran-e Sorkh ow Siyah" [Iran and the Red and Black Imperialists]. Its purpose was to mobilize public opinion against Ayatollah Khomeini, then exiled in Paris. The article, which called Khomeini a "troubadour", among other things, triggered riots the day after it was published in the city of Qom, which were soon followed by further uprisings in Tabriz and elsewhere. This was the beginning of the sequence of events that culminated just over a year afterwards in the monarchy's downfall.]

[13]On September 16, 1941 (20 Shahrivar, 1320), Reza Shah left Bandar Abbas for Johannesburg, forced into exile by the British. Leonard Binder writes, "In Shahrivar 1320...the myth of the national army was destroyed by the extremely poor showing made by the Iranian forces against British and Soviet allies." Iran: Political Development in a Changing Society (Berkeley: The University of California Press, 1964), p. 144. On August 19, 1953 (28 Mordad) the famous CIA-backed coup took place, ousting the nationalist Mossadeq government and reinstalling the shah. See Cottam, op. cit., pp. 225-29. (tr)

[14]In 1837-1838, Muhammad Shah, encouraged and assisted by the Russian army, unsuccessfully beseiged Herat. The victorious Afghani defenders, led by Yar

Muhammad Khan, were aided and supported by the British. (tr)

¹⁵Fayziyeh Madraseh is one of the Islamic semi-
naries in the city of Qom. Al-e Ahmad is alluding to
the government's use of commandos to occupy the
school and quell student uprisings there in early
June of 1963, on the fifteenth of Khordad [June 5]
and the days following. (tr)

¹⁶In the interval between the first and second
editions of this booklet the Ministry of Education,
with much propaganda and fanfare, created the Sepah-e
Danesh [Literacy Corps], for which it selects high
school graduates by lottery to be sent to the villages in military uniform to teach instead of simple
military service after four months' service in the
ranks, with a salary of 150 tumans [$21.43] per
month. So far they've run through two or three
cycles, and in each of our cycles two- to three-
thousand 'literacy corpsmen' have been sent to the
village, with elaborate exhibitions in the cities and
villages. On the surface this is a useful thing to
do, which will prevent a small number of this swarm
of high school graduates (which number twenty
thousand annually) from wasting their time, but the
most significant thing it really accomplishes is to
militarize education in the country. Whether it's
something to be proud of or treason, it was initiated
by Dr. Parviz Natel Khanlari, formerly a poet, later
a senator, and currently Minister of Education!
These Ministry of Education measures would have been
useful if they'd been carried out under the supervi-
sion of the teachers' colleges rather than under the
shadow of the army, and had they accepted a larger
number of volunteers and exempted them from serving
in the army. In any case, in the view of this
writer, and for the reasons given below these
measures were very detrimental in practice:

A - With such a plan they've placed the burden
of that thirty percent they cut out of the Ministry
of War's budget under pressure from American policy
onto the back of the Ministry of Education.

B - The teaching profession, which had just
begun to gain greater respect after the salary increases of 1341 [Mar 21 1962-Mar 20 1963] (during the
time of [Mohammad] Derakhsesh's ministry, based on a
minimum salary of 500 tumans [$71.43]), was again
made disreputable when it became associated with

underutilized manpower in the army.

C - The Ministry of Education, which was the government institution farthest removed from military activity, has in this way been placed under the army's spurs. (A)

''This chapter went very differently from this point on in the Muslim Student's Association edition: /We'll be able to discuss Western democracy in this country only when the preliminary obstacles have been overcome./

/Among these are powerful local leaders and big landowners. The remnants of the feudal system and tribal governments have always obstructed freedom and self determination for the people. If we were to grant all the people the right to vote tomorrow, in the end the ones to receive their votes would be the people who gave them per diem allowances to go to the polls or provided free transportation there, to say nothing of the mayors, gendarmes, governors, and district governors, all of them uncrowned shahs in their respective provinces or villages./

/A nation that has grown a certain way for thousands of years, that has been governed by self-serving leaders and fostered individualism throughout this long period, that has grown accustomed to hypocrisy and immersed itself in anachronisms and superstition, that fears everything and has always had its aspirations blocked by feudal lords and boss rule, and had its self-confidence destroyed by dictators--assuming that it was allowed to express its inner feelings in political matters--would never go to the polls. We haven't even taught the people the difference between Hassan and Hossein, or what it means to express an opinion at the ballot box. Could such an election be anything more than an election by a rabble, in the most direct sense of the word?/

/Our freedom has been limited throughout the short interval since the twentieth of Shahrivar, and we've tasted no more of it than I've indicated. These unpleasant consequences have themselves provided reasons for the current government to look to serving its own interests. As long as machines and industry have not regimented the people, as I will discuss later, and accustomed them to political parties, and as long as the concept of democracy has not penetrated to the core of our society through a

continuous training program, and as long as we can
only affect Western democracy, talk of Western
freedoms in this country is only fit for the company
of privileged individuals who sit around on regal oc-
casions with full stomachs and empty heads talking
pompously. As long as things stand as I see them
now, none of the seventy-five percent of our people
who are rural will even comprehend the meaning of the
anniversary celebration of the Constitutional Revolution on the fourteenth of Mordad./

[Translators' note: On August 18, 1906 (14
Mordad), a month-long protest by the 'ulama ended
with a triumphant mass march into Tehran, and the
granting of a constitution. See Algar, op. cit.,
chapter 14, for an analysis of those events.]

ARDESHIR 82

9

WHAT ARE OUR SCHOOLS AND UNIVERSITIES DOING?

Let's look at our society now from the point of view of education, a point of view that has always been my frame of reference. From the standpoint of education we're undisciplined, like wild grass. There is earth, a seed brought there by the wind or on a bird's beak, and rain helping the grass to grow. Just this way, *a plant's existence, and left to accident and wildness as well.* In like fashion, we build a school any way we can, to raise the property values in a neighborhood, to enhance the prestige of some powerful landowner, to redress the grievances arising from some bully's plundering in some political situation, through the honest efforts of the inhabitants of a village, with the endowment[1] of a third of someone's estate, by any means whatever, in any manner.

In any case, once the school is built, our educational network invariably takes hold of it with one of its brittle, inelastic branches, *and with such bustling around and so many headaches.* There's no previous plan whatever, no consideration of where schools are needed and where schools are superfluous. The concern for quantity still prevails over the wise minds in the Ministry of Education.

And the ultimate aim in the Ministry of Educa-

tion? *As I said*, the aim is to nurture **Gharbzadegi**,
or to place *worthless* certificates of employability
in the hands of people who are only fit to serve as
future stuffing for bureaucracies, and who need a
diploma for promotion to any position. There's no
coordination in the schools, of which we have every
variety: religious schools, Islamic schools,
/secular schools,/ *Italian schools, German schools,*
and schools that turn out pseudoclergymen and
theological students. We have technical and trade
schools, and a legion of other kinds, but the utility
of all this diversity, the reason for the existence
of each one of these schools, what they're cultivat-
ing, or what work their graduates take on /ten years
later/ is nowhere established or recorded. *Diversity
in itself--if it be in the sense of division of labor
and response to the people's diversity, skills,
taste, capability, and perception--is quite useful
and is itself the ultimate mark of freedom. But the
diversity in our schools is a kind of wildness, like
a seed that's planted just anywhere and left to come
up any way it can. There's a world of difference between state schools and private schools, and between
those in the provinces and the ones in Tehran, even
with the same program and the same teacher, for example. But in the one, there are eighty people per
class while the other has twenty-five. And so on.*

There is no evidence of reliance on tradition in
any school, no sign of the culture of the past, none
of the elements of morality or philosophy, not a sign
there of literature, no continuity between yesterday
and tomorrow, /between the home and tradition,/
between the home and the school, *between East and
West*, or between the individual and society! How can
a tradition that we've watched collapse lifelessly
have any effect on school programs? How can a home
whose foundations are in the process of disentegrat-
ing *serve as a foundation for our schools*, /schools
that don't know what they want?/ But every year, no
matter what, we turn out twenty-thousand new high
school graduates, bait for a future of every possible
complex, pressure, crisis, and rebellion. They're
irresponsible people with no ambition or drive, un-
resisting tools of governments, all willing to play
along with anything, *timid and idle*.

This may be the reason the Islamic schools have
suddenly acquired such luster in the last ten years.
At least in this type of school there's no perceived
danger to the faith and religion of the children, *who*

come from strict religious families and haven't yet
been hardened to the poisonous essence of
Gharbzadegi. But to what avail, since the rigidity
of the religious environment will harden them in
another way? This makes little difference, however,
when this problem of religion or the lack of it and
education or the lack of it are only problems in
/our/ cities. These concerns are the pastimes of urbanites, while out of fifty-thousand villages in our
nation, forty-thousand are without schools of any
kind.¹ I wish the ones that do have them did not,
because if the problem were universal at least there
would be a common calamity [illiteracy] everywhere.
As it stands now, there are a thousand problems,
everywhere different.

There are problems with textbooks; the shortage
of teachers; crowded classes; age differences among
the students; differences in intelligence, language,
and religion: teachers that may or may not be
schooled in the methods of teaching and training; the
tomb-like nature of the school buildings; the lack of
determination in their exercise and music programs,
and thousands of other problems.' The most important
problem of all is the Ministry of Education's aim-
lessness, and the program confusion. It still isn't
clear what the elementary schools must be set aside
for, for what aim, and to prepare for what skills.
And what about the high schools? And the universities? God save us from these universities! They
ought to be the liveliest and most prominent centers
of scientific, technical, and literary research.
Permit me to address myself briefly to these universities.

We have the University of Tehran, we have the
National University, the University of Shiraz, and
the ones in Khorasan and Jendi Shapur, and so on.
The National University is a storefront for that
group of Weststruck intellectuals who've returned
from Europe and America and heard so many moans and
groans about the University of Tehran's practices and
traditions that have already rigidified that they
went and opened a shop of their own relying on support from people in higher positions. I even find it
difficult to apply the name 'university' to this institution.

As for the colleges and universities in the
provinces, there was a time when a [Jafar] Pishevari
built the University of Tabriz in Azarbaijan as a

symbol of that province's independence or autonomy in
matters of law pertaining to state and provincial organizations (of which there no longer remains a sign
or a trace). Later on, when the disturbances in
Azarbaijan died down, they realized that this one
legacy of that facility couldn't be closed down with
curses and abuse like other elements of our heritage,
and that it couldn't be preserved either, because
whatever else it was it was a remnant left by the
Azarbaijan Democratic Party scenario.[1] So what
could we do? How about building universities in the
other provinces too.... So this is how we came to
have all these universities we have now. And how
nice, of course. At least work has been found for
all these candidates for professorships returning
from the West. But what are they going to do? No
one knows this yet. And in what field does each one
specialize? And of which specialized fields are the
provinces most in need? And which ones excel better
than the others? And what do they produce? Only God
knows when all these questions will be answered.   As
for the University of Tehran, with all its record of
achievement and importance, and all its vanished
traditions and shattered independence--whatever else
it may be, you would think it ought to be, as was
said, a center for the liveliest, most prominent, and
highest research. But is it?

Those university departments concerned with
technology, techniques, and machines (the colleges of
science and technology) merely produce good repairmen
for Western industrial products at the highest
academic levels--no new research, no discoveries, no
inventions, no problem solving, nothing. Just people
who keep Western industrial machines and products
running, put them to use and start them up, or people
who calculate the resistance of materials and this
kind of rubbish. And if there is just a little bit
of scientific research and investigation going on
it's at the Razi Institute and the Institute Pasteur,
which I don't know whether to consider a branch of
the University and College of Agriculture or the Ministry of Health or of the central Institute Pasteur
in Paris.

Perhaps it may be said that the medical colleges
can hold their own among other medical colleges at
the international level. But we must be quick to add
that they owe their excellence to the very high rates
of death and disease in these provinces. I have a
physician friend who studied in France. When it was

time for them to study the effects of the regional
Aleppo boil affliction the professor and his assistants looked everywhere and couldn't find anyone with
an Aleppo boil scar, until finally that friend himself showed them one on his own face, and they settled for seeing that for their familiarization with
this native disease. Here, however, God knows whose
unclaimed corpses have fallen into the hands of every
medical student! Therefore I'm certain that a medical student in Tehran or Shiraz or any other city in
Iran comes out of school with a lot more experience
and a lot more surgery and dissection under his belt
than the medical students in Europe or America, for
example. This is a strong point for Iranian medical
students that depends on the weak point of unusually
high rates of death and disease.

As for those university departments that have
nothing to do with science and technology, or that
deal with art and literature, such as the colleges of
fine arts and the colleges of literature (in Tehran
and the provinces), or with Islamic architecture and
Iranian culture, and research and investigation concerning them, I'll take them up one by one:

The colleges of fine arts, with only the two
fields of painting and architecture, are the only
university institutions that generally train artists.
If they can train artists. But the output of these
artists may be seen with a casual survey of the doors
and walls of the art galleries that are becoming
fashionable these days and also with a quick trip
down any alley or street. Minus a few exceptions,
the result of most of their efforts is the consumption of paints, stone, glass, and iron. Again, this
means consuming Western manufactures. Rarely is
anyone found among the Iranian artists and architects
who doesn't imitate Westerners and whose works have
that feature which is genuine and new and which adds
something to the world's collective art endeavors.
Things have even gotten to the point that we import a
judge and a critic from the West to judge painters. [4]

As for the colleges of literature, as it turns
out not only is nothing said about literature in the
true and universal sense, but even contemporary Persian literature remains unseen and unknown there.
The style of thinking of the late 'Abbas Eqbal still
prevails in these colleges. Eqbal, may God rest his
soul, showed how to see, recognize, and judge literature up to one-hundred years ago, but from then on?

Never.' *The result of this sort of approach to*
literature is that we merely train grave openers, and
because of this our colleges of literature ought to
be grouped with the colleges that deal with Islamic
law and science and Iranian culture and do their in-
vestigation and research in these matters, meaning
the colleges of law, philosophy, and the religious
sciences.

They're just like the Islamic schools, *mentioned*
previously,/ which have /thoughtlessly imagined to
themselves that they'll arrest the dangers of irreligion, which is only one of the symptoms of
<u>Gharbzadegi,</u> merely by /protecting,/ teaching, and
propagating religion *and religious principles.* *Our*
colleges of literature, law, and the religious scien-
ces have also imagined that they will forestall the
same danger by taking refuge in Arabic language and
1iterature, and oral and religious traditions. This
is why the colleges of literature, with all *the*
merits of their scholars, dissipate all their care
and energy opening graves, searching deeply into the
past, and researching the narrated traditions of
such-and-such and so-and-so!

In colleges of this type, on the one hand a
direct reaction to <u>Gharbzadegi</u> can /clearly/ be seen
in this retreat into old texts, old historical
figures and the dead glories of literature and
/mysticism;/*and abandoning the living present of*
today, and on the other hand the greatest manifestation of the ugliness of <u>Gharbzadegi</u> may be seen in
their professors' use of the work of orientalists, of
whose virtues I've spoken earlier, in their documentation.

When an educated, responsible man of tradition
who's a college professor intellectually involved
with law and literature *and Islamic and Iranian*
studies sees how the West's assault and its industrial products and technology are sweeping everything up and carrying it away, he imagines--*as a*
means of self-defense and self-expression--that the
more <u>Kalileh</u> <u>and</u> <u>Demneh'</u> experts he produces, the
better! This is why the graduates of this kind of
college have been so ineffectual in society during
the last twenty to thirty years, and why they've for-
feited their positions to people returning from the
West *and been left behind.* And may God grant long
lives to *their excellencies* the orientalists, who've
written an encyclopedia about every <u>Ilahi</u> <u>Nameh'</u> and

a dictionary on every book about some Sufi's beard just to keep these *Kalileh* and *Demneh* experts busy talking about form and essence, occurring and preexistence, the principle of innocence, and so on...

With a few minor exceptions, the graduates of the past twenty or thirty years from these colleges have been esteemed scholars and philologists. They all know a little bit about important political figures, and all are idiosyncratic commentators on other people's books and unravelers of abstruse etymological or historical problems. They are all certifiers of the true ownership of unmarked graves, exposers of falsely attributed literary works and of the theft or borrowing of such-and-such from so-and-so *one-thousand years ago,* or treatise writers about poets of the tenth century A.H., of whom there are no more than the number of fingers on both hands. Worst of all are those who teach literature in the high schools or are educational or school administrators, or *judges. And again, God bless those in this last group, who have sworn themselves to independence of judgment in the Ministry of Justice, and, if fortune is with them, can distinguish between the true and the false. But those others?* What good have they done us, after all? Other than going deeper into Gharbzadegi?

Every one of these professors *and their proteges* has so retired into his cave of old texts, scribes, and quotations, deaf as the Seven Sleepers of Ephesus, that nothing, not even an automobile horn, will arouse him. They even plug up their ear canals with these very manuscripts to avoid hearing the ugly sound of those horns. /They're all just another manifestation of Gharbzadegi, or a big indication of it. Here, cause and effect are inseparable. It's the chicken and egg again. I will leave it./

Day by day, the mastery of foreign tongues is taking the place of the mother tongue in importance and need for us. Day by day the fields of science and technology are taking people away from these fields and reducing the number of people interested in them. Iranian and Islamic ethics, mores, and sciences, as we've observed throughout the booklet, are becoming more remote and worthless every day. And then in a situation like this the country's centers of literature, law, and learning, the colleges of literature, law, and the Islamic sciences, just as the clergy, which has taken refuge in the cocoon of prejudice and rigidity in the face of the West's assault, have taken refuge in the cocoon of old texts and contented themselves with training people who search for dots and strokes. These days, just as the clergy has become mired in discussions about what to do when in doubt about which prostration comes next in the prayer ritual, and expounding on what is and is not ritually clean, the centers of literature, law, and Iranian, Eastern, and Islamic studies of this kind are also mired in discussion about the decorative [Arabic] letter 'b' and whether it ought to be connected [to the next letter] or not, and about the silent [Persian] 'v' and whether it ought to be deleted [in writing] or not. This is the very truth. When you throw a man out of the world at large he'll start grasping at details. Yes. When a flood carries the house away or it collapses in an earthquake, you go searching through the debris for a loose door so you can carry the decomposed corpse of a dear one to the graveyard on it.

With regard to educational and university issues, another big problem is the problem of this flood of returnees from Europe and America, all of whom have returned at the very least as candidates for a ministry job, but ended up as governmental deadweight. They're undoubtedly a windfall for us, like an odd shoe in the desert, but be realistic and look at what garbage every one of these windfalls turns out to be after coming back and finding a place in an organization and becoming established. They have no area of expertise, no work to do, and no ability to get anything done. They are neither generous nor wholehearted, and most of them are irresponsible. Especially since even those in this group also consider themselves and their opinions to be worthless alongside those of the Western consultants and advisors who dominate the situation. /They're perfect examples of culturally transplanted Gharbzadegi, a people with their feet in the air, transmitters of the opinions of foreign advisers and experts./ Contrary to its reputation, and in my view, the larger this group of returnees from abroad becomes, the less it accomplishes, and the greater is the helplessness and discord within the organization under its influence!

On the one hand there was never any plan about where to send these young people, and for what specializations, professions, and technologies.

Every young person of this kind has gone to some part of the world of his or her own choosing and desire, each has studied something and experienced something completely different from the other. Now that they've returned, each one a candidate for employment in one of the country's governmental agencies or organizations, it will become clear how inept they are and how powerless to do anything! *The one who was trained in France differs from the one trained in England, Germany or America. Each one winds up the instrument differently and plays it a different way. But let me add this point here also, that if I see reasons to be hopeful for the future of intellectualism in Iran, one of the reasons is this very diversity of training and in the academic roots and backgrounds of our people who've been to Europe. The wellspring of the wealth of Iran's intellectual environment is right here. Look at at India's intellectual environment and how they affect Britishness, with the majority of them Oxford graduates! In any case, there are a great many points concerning these people who've returned from Europe and America. It's best to enumerate them one by one.*

The first point is that in the country's current circumstances, most of of these young people are exactly like the beautiful tulips, narcissus, and hyacinths whose bulbs we import from Holland and nurture in Tehran greenhouses until they bloom. Then we buy a flower pot for them at an enormous price and bear it as a gift for this friend or that acquaintance, and even though the friend keeps them in a warm sunlit room, they don't even last another week! These choice blossoms of our society will likewise wilt in the climate of this country. We've seen them and had experience with them, and if they don't wilt /in most cases, make no mistake about it,/ they'll /have to/ go along with the tide.

Contrary to all this propaganda about bringing back the students who've gone to the West, I don't think there's any hope of their being of service to the country when they come back until there's a receptive environment in these provinces for their activities of the future.

And so the question arises, who will be the one to prepare this environment? You can see that there are many issues. I think that in this bitter cold place the ones who will be able to prepare the way will have simmered in the ovens here and learned the

ropes in these cold climes. /As long as the condition of our Western-educated students remains as
we've seen, with all this disharmony we have, and
study in the West is left up to individual desire,
accident, and circumstance, I don't think there's
much hope for us, despite [what they say]. that the
more Western-educated people we have, the more hope
there is for success in renovating the structure of
our country./*

A second point is that most of these young
people, when they live in Europe or America and imitate free societies and environments to varying
degrees, have a certain understanding of freedom and
create a stir of activity in their student unions.
Most of them are hot and full of vim and vigor. And
talk, activities, demonstrations, and publications.
As soon as they return, however, and they get hold of
the cow's tail here, all those factors are forgotten.
Yes, it may be that the passing of youth, which is
accompanied by fire and passion, is one of the
reasons for this forgetting. But don't you think
that such a regression occurs here because the
governments don't encourage that kind of talk and
such freedoms aren't permitted? In any event,
whatever the reason, I know a whole string of young
people like this, each one of whom has retired into a
corner after coming back and contented himself with
having whatever might come his way from this feast.
You wouldn't think they'd been rebellious and
liberationist at one time. A wife, the responsibilities of life, and children are also ready ex-
cuses. Especially if the wife is a Westerner.

The third point is in fact this very issue, the
very fact that a significant number of young men like
this come back with European and American wives, and
there's also a very small number of girls who come
back with European or American husbands. And don't
you think that this is itself another problem added
to all the other problems? When the basis of the
Iranian family with a close and familiar wife and
husband of the same blood is falling apart, of course
it's obvious what must be happening in this sort of
mismatched family. These young people and their
families are like homing pigeons with two roosts.
They are the ultimate human results of <u>Gharbzadegi</u>.
To solve the domestic difficulties in a family like
this is itself enough of a problem. This group of
young people has neither the ability nor the ambition
to solve the external, or social problems. There are

no more than two or three categories of young people
of this type:

   A - Those who came from poor families and got
themselves to the West with difficulty and studied.
For this group, having a European or American wife or
husband is a way to break with lineage and blood
ties, which no longer constitute a suitable milieu
for a dignitary returned from the West, and a ladder
to pull oneself up from its level to a higher social
level. The dangerous consequences of a marriage like
this are plainer than day.'

   B - Those who settled for marrying a Western
woman or man because of the rigid and onerous marriage restrictions and regulations in Iran. And now
that they have returned with knowledge, diplomas, and
the ability to speak European languages, they find
that all those restrictions are broken and it seems
as if they've brought back a European woman or man
souvenir for nothing. The consequences of such a
situation with the comparisons that will face them
later are also clear.

   C - Those who (whether girls or boys) lose their
virginity in Europe or America and begin womanizing
or carousing with men among the Europeans and later
upon returning with a foreign mate either no longer
recognize any God and find no one acceptable, or
realize how wrong they were, and so on like this....

   In each of these instances or others, when a
young Iranian graduate comes back with a European or
American mate, the explanation given for it will fall
back on these two or three points:

   He has either married a foreigner when that foreigner's environment or that environment of foreigners accepted him (for example because of the
shortage of men in Germany after the war--this is the
very reason why the percentage of German women who
have married Iranians is more than any other
nationality of women). And isn't this being accepted
in a foreign environment and by a foreign woman in
reality the same as being uprooted from one's own native environment? And won't this in itself lead to a
sort of chronic manpower shortage for us? And of
trained and educated manpower at that? In any case,
where the girls that marry foreign husbands are concerned we lose them all with very few exceptions.

*Or for this reason, that the young Iranian
graduate in Europe or America wanted to compensate
for the pain of the contempt that dogged his or her
steps while he or she compared all aspects of Iran
with Europe and America and in his or her environment
and manners, etc.... I'll say that in confidence and
pass on.*[10]

With this information don't you think that
taking a Western husband or wife is itself one of the
most acute instances of the emergence of <u>Gharbzadegi</u>?
If this is the case I think the time has come for us
to send students to India and Japan for higher education and nowhere else *in Europe or America*, with a
/clear and/ orderly plan *appropriate to the country's
technical and scientific needs*, for a period of say
twenty years or so. I say only these two countries
because we all know how they've come to terms with
machines, how they've taken hold of technology (*especially Japan*) and how they've dealt with the problems
we now face. In my estimation, only when such a plan
or plans of this nature have been put into effect
will it be possible to be hopeful for the future of
our education, through the establishment of an equi-
librium between the Eaststruckness(!) of the Asia
returnees and the <u>Gharbzadegi</u> of present-day returnees from the West.[11]

NOTES

[1]The Persian word is <u>vaqf</u>, meaning mortmain, an inalienable endowment, legacy, or bequest of a pious or religious nature, established for religious or charitable purposes. (tr)

[2]*The Literacy Corps claims that it now has temporary schools operating in ten-thousand villages despite all its public relations hustling, and this apart from all the liabilities I've already discussed. This is good news in any event.* (A)

[3]Jafar Pishevari was leader of the Democratic Party of Azarbaijan, which was the organizing force for the Azarbaijan seperatist movement in the early 1940s. Pishevari was also prime minister of Azarbaijan during its brief period of autonomy between September 1945 and December 1946. (tr)

[4]*Concerning the output of these painters, see* Keyhan's Ketab-e Mah *in the two issues (the first one and the final one) for Khordad [May 22-June 21] and Shahrivar [Sep 23-Oct 22] of 1341 [1962] and the various articles by Simin Danishvar and Jalal Moqadam, and the article on the painters' conference.*

[5]*See the issues of the magazine* Yadgar *from the period when that late gentleman ran it.* (A)

[6]Known also as Bidpai, or A Mirror for Princes, Kalileh and Demneh is a collection of Indian fables dating to the early fourth century A.D. Kalileh and Demneh are corruptions of the Sanskrit names of the two principal characters, two jackals, Karataka and Damanaka, counselors to the lion king. The work is a frame story containing numerous fables designed to teach political wisdom or cunning. (tr)

[7]See Farid al-Din Attar, 13th cent., The Ilahinama, or Book of God, translated by John Andrew Boyle (Manchester, England: Manchester University Press, 1976). (tr)

[8]To see how this chapter ended in the Muslim Students' Association edition, read the following transitional paragraph (deleted in the Ravaq edition) and go to the last paragraph in the chapter. (tr)

/This line of reasoning is what leads me to believe that it's time we totally refrained from sending students to Europe and America. We've seen what results all this study in Europe and America does and does not produce./

*A popular belief concerning this unpopular phenomenon is that whenever a man attains a position, if he has a European or American wife everyone will know it was only because of having a Western wife that he got the position, even though the man himself has the highest qualifications. (A)

[10]I came across this point when the book Les Quarantaines by Fereydoun Hoveyda came out (in French, in 1341) [1962], explaining it. A very nice young Easterner (Fereydoun cast himself as a Lebanese/Egyptian in that book, and it makes no difference) in the confrontation between East and West-- and in a spiritual confrontation between these two worlds within himself--triumphs over his psychological problems and his embarrassment and feelings of contemptibility when he wins a European woman who had captured his heart several years earlier. A more interesting point in this book is that, even with the feeling of love after the object of desire was obtained, and before as well, the hero of the book didn't have the courage to articulate this love, even secretly to himself. (A)

[11]A study of the structure and history of Iranian education was published the same year the first edition of Gharbzadegi appeared in Persian. See Reza Arasteh, Education and Social Awakening in Iran (Leiden: 1962). (tr)

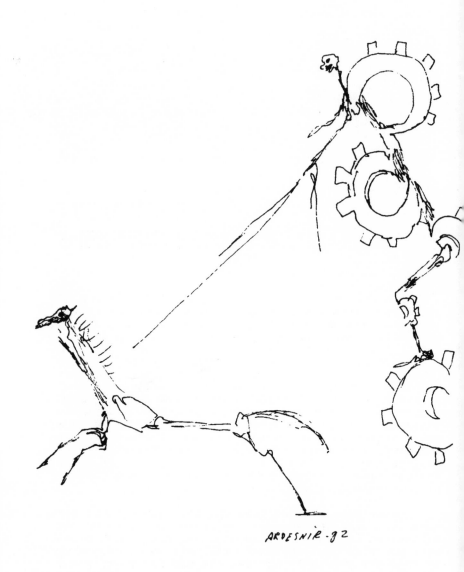

ARDESHIR - 82

10

A BIT ABOUT
MACHINESTRUCKNESS

The prominent factors distinguishing this era of confusion, with its characteristic crises, are scientific advances on one side; changes in technology, the arts, and machinery on another; and on another side the possibility of discussing Western democracies.[1] We only have these three factors (*scientific advances, changes in technology, the possibility of discussing freedom*) in superficial form. *We have samples we can use to show off.* If the rapid evolution of machines *and technology* to increase production brings on social crisis,[2] for us, who are only beginning now and must cross a two-hundred-year time lag, this process will ultimately bring on more devastation than we can imagine, and our own fever and delirium will be even more hopeless and interminable than that of other similar nations.

Nevertheless, let's assume that tomorrow we become like Switzerland, Sweden, France or the United States--an impossible assumption is not impossible-- what would we be like then? Wouldn't we be caught up in the same problems the West has had *for some time*? What would we do about these new problems? Before I discuss one or two of these kinds of problems, let me say that my purpose is to clarify the massive problems we have already, so we can see what a long way we have to go and what a vast void we must fill.

One basic problem with Western civilization in the Western nations themselves is the obligatory vigilance against the seeds of facism which is built into nineteenth-century liberalism. In France, we have *His Excellency Mr.* De Gaulle,[3] with the Algerian problem at his feet, and right-wing militant and nonmilitant extremists working hand in hand with the hoods of the Foreign Legion, who stain the streets of Paris and Algeria every day with the blood of those who are trying to solve Algeria's problems. In Italy and Germany we have the remnants of the Brownshirts, and in America we have a new /secret/ organization called the [John] Birch Society, which thinks even *His Excellency Mr.* Eisenhower is a communist. In England there's the Scotch /Republic/ Independence movement, and everywhere else the tree has a worm of the same proportions!

This Foreign Legion itself poses a problem of this nature for Europe. We know that every European criminal and exile, *and at least every adventurer,* when no longer able to remain in his own community because he has reached a dead end, is forced to volunteer for the legion, unless of course he goes to work for a *diamond or* gold-mining or ivory-trading company in the African jungles (see <u>Journey</u> <u>to</u> <u>the</u> <u>End</u> <u>of</u> <u>Night</u>, by Louis Ferdinand Celine, the late *contemporary* French writer).[4] Thus the Bandar Abbas of Belgium is the Congo, and the Qeshm Island[5] of France is Algeria, Djibouti, or Madagascar. For Italy it's Somalia or Libya, *for the Portuguese it's Angola or Mozambique,* and for the Dutch (the Boers who control South Africa are of Dutch extraction) it's South Africa *or Indonesia.*

What do you think this legion is, after all? It's something just like the old-time mercenary armies. What is its mission? To destroy freedom wherever necessary, to serve the oil and gold-mining companies wherever the local people make trouble, and to be a gang of mechanized (!) cutthroats for whichever bully pays the most money. Ever since Spain in 1936 and continuing until Algeria and the Congo *and Angola* just recently, *wherever the stage was set for depradation, gentlemen like these were there and everyone* got bloodied and pulverized under the bootheels of these European gangsters. And anyway the issue is not simply a matter of Europe exporting hoods along with its machines.[5] What's really significant is that Europe preserves the well-being and security of its cities, museums, and

theaters by depriving colonized and backward
countries of their freedom. Now that the colonized
nations are attaining their freedom one after
another, and we see that Europe cannot protect its
assets, let's see how Europe will cope with the 'un-
wanted merchandise' it has been left with. One may
assuredly expect to see a lot of chaos in Europe. *As
it appears on the surface, it seems that Angola,
Mozambique, and South Africa are still the principal
bases for these Foreign Legionnaires, and don't you
think that later on these gentlemen will change
clothes and come sit at the side of the Shaykh of
Kuwait as consultants, advisors, and experts, or become ministers to the Shaykh of Qatar, or even in our
own state? Let me move on.*

Why is this so? Why, in the heart of Western
civilization, do such difficulties become obstacles
in the pathway of every change? The reason, in my
mind, is that *adventurism, rebellion against the
people and the laws, intellectual and virtual
brutality, /and fascism/* are themselves the secondary
results of regimenting people alongside machines.
*The initial results are Western industrial products,
the secondary results are these things,* and this
regimentation is itself a machine requirement. *Cause
and effect are together.* Mechanized uniformity,
lining up in ranks at the factories, coming and going
on time, and doing one kind of *sickening* work
throughout life will become second nature to all
people who have anything to do with machines. At-
tending the meetings of political parties and unions,
where uniformity of dress, manners, greetings, and
thought are expected is a third habitual pattern that
will follow in the wake of machines.

Uniformity of dress in the factories, then, will
lead to uniformity in the political parties and
unions. This, in turn, will lead to uniformity in
the barracks--meaning alongside war machines! What
difference does it make? A machine is a machine.
One makes milk bottles for children, another makes
hand grenades for young and old, adults and children.
It is this uniformity of shape, *dress,* and thought in
the service of machines (*which Charlie Chaplin sharply condemned, and if we acknowledge his worth the
reason is that he perceived the danger of going to
the slaughterhouse of machines like sheep*), and in
the unions, *clubs,* and political parties and barracks
that leads to the uniformity of shape, *dress,* and
thought of the Black shirts and Brown shirts. And

every twenty years or so it draws these same Western *sheep for slaughter,* as we have seen, into bloodshed, when they call the world to war and relegate all these problems to the realm of memory. To put it more clearly, /fascism and/ war-mongering--*apart from the fact that they appear as the sequel to vigorous industrial expansion and the search for new markets to export goods*--basically derive their manners and customs from machines, machines that are themselves the harvest of 'pragmatism', 'scientism', 'positivism', and other similar 'isms', /both in the sense I have discussed and in the simple sense put forward in socialism/. *These days even children can see that* whenever machines have *reached the surplus production stage* and attained the capability of ex-porting *their manufactures, the owners of the machines (the companies)* have then entered into vi-cious hostilities with competitors *in order to monopolize the export markets.*'

In addition to these concerns, let's notice that the political parties in a Western democratic society are /actually/ pulpits for *giving satisfaction to the* deranged *emotions* of unstable, and--from the psychological standpoint--sick people, who have been deprived of any sort of opportunity to express them-selves because of the daily lineup *at the machine,* getting up exactly on schedule every day, *getting to* work, and not missing the street car, and also if we notice, the Fascist parties and other extremist par-ties, in their origins and their prejudiced deriva-tives, take the greatest pains to satisfy the sick desires of this very /type of/ human being, from the intensely red coloration they adopt for their flags to the insignias, signs, and symbols they employ using eagles, lions, and tigers, which are really the savage totems of the twentieth century, and their customs and ceremonies for entering and leaving their gatherings. *So we can see the first cause of these diseases and the way to either cure them or retain them chronically.* These are all problems of the West and the advanced machinestruck societies, solutions to which are the concern of the experts of those na-tions!

As for ourselves, we don't know about democracy, and we lack an understanding of machines that would enable us to comprehend the regimentation that goes with them. It's amusing that we have parties and societies, established by decree! Instead of being drawn into line by machines, and then being driven

from there to political parties and (democratic)
society, and then re-forming those same ranks in the
barracks, we have begun at the opposite end. First
we establish the ranks and the uniformity in the
military barracks (which are never used for *war--
except war in the streets*) so that when we do acquire
machines we won't be functioning improperly, or in
other words so that the machines won't be functioning
improperly. This is the best thing I can say about
our situation today. In the West they arrived at
regimentation, military barracks, and war by way of
machines and technology, while we were just the opposite. *From military barracks and training for
street fighting--we go to joining a party system and
becoming slaves to machines. That is, we're trying
to get there.* /This is unraveling the skein from the
center./ Enough said. /This is one point./

Another of the problems *Western societies have
is that the West, in the days when it had its
colonizing encounters with the East, Asia,* Africa,
and South America, was in totally different circumstances than it is today. The Western man of the
nineteenth century who came to this part of the world
along with the first industrial products did whatever
he wished to do. He was assistant to lords, princes,
and governors. He was advisor and consultant. He
sheltered advocates of the Constitutional Revolution
in his embassy *in Tehran,* and in Shiraz, during the
fighting between the Qashqa'is and the followers of
Qavam [al-Molk],' any house flying his flag above
its roof was safe, an inviolable refuge. Now,
however, when even the primitive people of the Congo,
because of the nationalization of oil, of the Suez
Canal and of the Cuban sugar companies, have studied
and learned *to recognize foreigners in any guise* and
not to take them in with such endearing hospitality,
the Westerner has changed his skin. He's put on a
new face so as not to be recognized.

If the Westerner *who came to Asia and the East*
was "Master" or "Sahib" and his wife "Mum Sahib" in
those early days, today he's a consultant or advisor
under the auspices of UNESCO. Though he's come here
to do the same *or similar* things, he dresses more ac-
ceptably. He no longer wears a safari hat (colonial
hat) and he watches his appearance. We Easterners
and Asians ourselves, however, haven't yet grasped
this point, now understood by Western man, that it
isn't possible to go back two-hundred years in the
second half of the twentieth century. We've not yet

understood that those scarecrows of the nineteenth century were those same 'pots over the head' we saw earlier.

Apart from all this, the colonizing Westerners sometimes brought along artists in their caravans, like Gauguin the painter, Joseph Conrad the writer, Gerard de Nerval, Pierre Lewis, /Somerset Maugham,/ and more recently, Andre Gide and Albert Camus... Each of these people became emotionally attached to some aspect of the virgin beauty of the East, and created works that shook the foundations of Western standards in life, art, and politics. Gauguin brought the essence of the sun and color to the West on his canvases, and so disrupted *the dark and gloomy painting of Flamand* that today the works of Picasso and Dali seem old-fashioned. In 1934, Gide, in his journals of the Congo, brutally shamed the world's marketplaces with his accounts of the ivory-trading and gold-mining companies. Andre Malraux provided information on Southeast Asian *Khmer* civilizations, which are older than the four pillars of the Forum of Rome or the Acropolis of Athens. There were others, all of whom, by seeking out the paths and customs of other lives in the East and *Asia or South America*, discovered worlds of which nothing was known *within the walled-in confines of* Europe and the West.

The story of jazz music is another kind of horn in itself. In the case of jazz, it is the black Africans who now wail beneath the skies of New York. This is the same black man who was once a slave growing cotton for aristocrats and Western companies *in New Jersey and Mississippi*, and who now shakes the ceilings of /Buckingham Palace, Windsor Castle, and/ Carnegie Hall with his trumpets and drums, and *in no time at all* he will be finding his way into Gothic churches, which have never opened their doors to any music except Bach and Mendelssohn.

I want to say that the West, in colonization's beginnings, merely sucked the East's blood--which included ivory, oil, silk, spices, and other material goods--like a leech. Now, however, it has gradually realized that the East, *apart from the material goods and what the museums and factories have brought from there*, also possesses an abundance of spiritual wealth, *that which the universities and laboratories are working with*. And as we saw, this was how the basis for anthropology, mythology, dialectology, and a thousand other 'ologies' based on gleanings from

*this very end of the world was planted in that end of
the world.* And now, in addition to all this,
/gradually/ the spiritual wealth of the East, of
Africa, and of South America has become a mental
preoccupation for ·Western intellectuals and educated
people. It has now come to the point where the
literate, cultivated man of the West enjoys 'primitive' African sculpture and jazz music. In literature he reads the Upanishads, Tagore, Taoism, Bud-
dism, and Zen. *Who is someone like Thomas Mann,
anyway? Or Herman Hesse? And what does existen-
tialism say?* Every young stripling in the West knows
the art of Japanese gardening, *how to drink tea
Chinese style,* and how to serve an Indian meal.

The Westerner's turning to Eastern *and African
criteria in art and literature and in life and ethics
(which shows on the one hand the Westerner's disgust
and at least weariness of his environment, customs,
and art, and on the other hand it shows how arts,
customs, and culture from anywhere can spread over
the entire world, and this is of course a very
beautiful sign)* is gradually extending into the
domain of politics. *And don't you think that, as a
follow-up to the West's attention to Eastern art, the
time has now come for the West to turn its attention
to Eastern politics?* Yes, the escape from
machinestruckness requires this. The fear of atomic
war dictates this.

At the same time, we Weststruck people in such
times don't know our own music and hear it as useless
noise. We talk about symphonies and rhapsodies.
We've turned our backs on Iranian portraiture and
miniatures. /Imitating the Venice Art Festival, we
paint heaps of color side-by-side,/ and in imitation
of the Biennale of Venice we even consider fauvism
and cubism out-of-date. We've laid Iranian architecture aside, with its symmetry, its ponds and foun-
tains; its gardens, basements, bathhouses; and sash
and latticed windows. We have closed our traditional
gymnasiums' and forgotten how to play polo. We take
four wrestlers to the Olympic games, which were
founded on the basis of the marathon,[10] itself a symbol of the defeat of a military despot of ancient
times who launched a campaign from this side of the
world to that side.

Why, after all, shouldn't Eastern nations be
aware of their own wealth? And why, just because
machines are Western, and we have to adopt them, have

we supplanted all our /Eastern/ criteria for life,
manners, and art with Western ones? Why should the
UNESCO emblem be designed after the Greek columns of
the Acropolis? And not, for example, after the As-
syrian winged bull, or the columns of the Egyptian
temples at Karnak and Abu Simbel? Why shouldn't
Eastern countries, for example, take their own
national games to the Olympics? /Polo, for example,
or horse racing,/ archery, dancing, physical exercises (I mean yoga) or /Iranian calisthenics/.

Enough. This is another point.

/A further point is that if machine service requires pliable, submissive, and normal people whose
problems, discomforts, and pacification are all
handled by the political parties on the rostrum, who
have passed some intelligence test, whose pulses beat
so many times per minute, who are of a certain height
and who turn their wrenches so many times a minute
lest their machines be ruined or damaged and the company's capital be wasted--and Western education and
training seeks and selects such men for that
purpose--and the Ford Motor Company, for example,
tells the University of Chicago that it wants two-
thousand of a certain type of person graduated in
electrical engineering during the next ten years
towards the same end--I don't know why we, who have
no machines and no compelling need to produce submissive, pliable, identical people, are seeking these
same stable people in our education who are adjusted
a certain way and have a certain type of
tolerance,/ I'll move on.

Another problem for Western societies is that in
addition to the submissive and compliant people they
create--for the purpose of serving machines--they
also create people of a new variety who may be
characterized as 'made-to-order heroes', just like
prefabricated houses, in the larger-than-life images
of cinema stars, or in those who ride in the noses of
rockets. This, of course, is also logical. When
you've made all the people into a single piece of
canvas from one end to the other with not a one of
them sticking his head up above the others, there is
no alternative but to break up this uniformity of
common humanity and present an example so the hope-
lessness won't be absolute. This is how it happens
that while, for example, the Ford Company orders so
many electrical and mechanical specialists from such-
and-such a university every year with such-and-such

characteristics, such-and-such a film company is also
doing its work, that is, it's creating heroes, according to a plan. Although there was a time when a
certain specified kind of courage (which, as Plato
said, was one of the four virtues) would emerge from
someone spontaneously and that person became a hero
and the poets sang his praises, now such-and-such a
film company calls for someone to act out such-and-
such a historical or legendary act of courage in order to make some film, and come look at how the
newspapers, radio, and television carry on about it.
And the companies promote it in every possible way,
spend a fortune on publicity, and dramatize the lives
of their stars, their marriages and divorces, their
children being kidnapped, their participation in some
black-and-white struggle, their dancing on such-and-
such a night with some divorced queen, and so on....
And for a year or two before the film is finished it
continually comes out and comes out in the
newspapers, radio, and television to the point that
news of it by way of Reuter and the Associated Press
even reaches the ears of the media in Tehran, Sin-
gapore, and Khartoum. Then the time is ripe and the
film has an awesome, almighty opening night in one of
the fifteen capitals of the world, attended by dig-
nitaries of state and so on. And the result?
Another hero is added to the list of screen heroes,
which is to say that in reality another historical
and legendary hero has had his prestige and
credibility damaged.

Another example of this kind of hero making--
that is, the ordinary man becoming a hero on the
screen--is those men who ride in the noses of space
rockets, whose wives didn't even take them seriously
until yesterday, or who weren't even married, but
today they're famous from horizon to horizon. And in
what situation? In a situation where the scientists
who built the rockets themselves and the principal
discoverers of the new fuels for space travel live in
complete anonymity. Both in the Soviet Union and the
United States. And why? Because the names and backgrounds of the rocket builders, even their human existence, are military secrets not to be divulged.
But the one who rides in the rocket? Of course it's
no secret. It's a way to make fools of the people, a
tear someplace in this featureless, mundane expanse
which is the fate of the vast masses, in order to
raise some hope in their hearts that says "yes, you
too could have been a rocket man," and so on. And
then so many photographs and details, so many com-

memorative stamps, so many press releases, and so
much garbage! And with such propaganda and maneuvering! Heedless of the fact that he's a human being
like all the others, with a bit more courage and perhaps a bit more luck, since we know nothing of the
fate of those who have been annihilated in space.
It's a military secret, after all! And in any case,
don't you think that such an astronaut, while being a
human being with all the rights of one, has also become something like a laboratory rabbit in this
space-travel experiment? This is a degradation of
humanity! The gentlemen themselves don't hide it,
saying "yes, such-and-such an astronaut is so brave,"
and so on, and "he's ready to sacrifice his life for
humanity"! And I say it's for technical progress!
After all, there was a time when His Holiness Abraham
brought his son for sacrifice in the name of God, but
today they sacrifice people for technology and
machines. And they're proud of it too! And they've
done such trumpeting and bugling in both directions
for astronauts that you see legions of people in
every Siberian or Alaskan village who are signing up
or have signed up for this sacrifice. And isn't this
in itself a sort of flight from monotony that
machines impose on people? In any case, this is the
machine's ultimate violence in the domain of
humanity!

At first they wrote things making fun of space
rockets that we would read, saying "yes, they pinned
Christ down in the fourth heaven with a needle and
now the rockets are navigating the seventh heaven,"
and things of this nature. This humor was used to
conceal the reality that even the heavens are no
longer the domain of the angels. And it's all human
nature. A human nature that will rise above the fir-
mament if it goes into the service of machines, and
other such propaganda, ignoring the fact that monkeys
and dogs preceded this degraded humanity in this
celestial wandering. In any case, you can see that
in the industrial countries it's no longer a question
of machines wanting submissive and compliant people
with such-and-such qualifications. Rather the point
is that, in making such human sacrifices, machines
are creating a new kind of human being. They
diminish the dignity of mankind by taking sacrifices
from it with the same status as four-legged animals.
In the news item "such-and-such a rocket lady marries
a handsome young rocket man," and the sequel, "the
lady is pregnant now," followed by "astronaut couple
has baby," I see humanity itself being toyed with,

and pragmatism and scientism being carried to the
point that they put the two human sexual beings
through difficult experiments like two mice, then
they fertilize and breed them... For what? To prove
that a human being can breed in outer space too. And
then what? This is the question! Let me move on.
In any case, these things are problems for the advanced societies. What we already know about this is
enough. But we, who neither have machines nor an advanced society; ought not to get wrapped up in these
consequences I've listed; have no compelling need to
create submissive, compliant people; and have no need
of made-to-order heroes--come look and see what we
won't do! We make these same myth-making claims
about people who win prizes, or during the election
of parliamentary representatives, or in the election
of such-and-such a villager who's to read at such-
and-such a poetry event, and so on like this.... And
worst of all is that we see the training of these
same stable individuals and other uselessness on the
front page of every educational assembly program....
Of course it can be protested that this, too, is
another sign of _Gharbzadegi_, but is it enough just to
give the pain a name? I'll comment in somewhat
greater detail concerning the most dangerous effect
of machinestruckness that has emerged in the Ministry
of Education. Solution

If one were to designate a proper role for our
educational system, it ought to be to discover out-
standing people who are ultimately able to lead this
caravan somewhere in the midst of this social chaos
caused by the crisis of Gharbzadegi. Such as it is,
the Ministry of Education's aim must not be and cannot be to make human beings identical and all of a
piece, so they all tolerate the present situation and
learn to live with it. Especially for us who are
living in this time of change and crisis. In an age
of social hell such as the one we're now passing
through it will only be possible to endure all this
change and crisis and to restore order to all this
social disorder we have seen in this book with the
help of people who are /dedicated,/ principled, and
self-sacrificing (these people are called "stubborn"
and "willful" and unstable in popular psychological
jargon).

If it was true at one time that this country's
aristocratic educational system was only used to
train the country's leaders, as in the Safavid or
Qajar periods or before, when teaching and training

*were precisely coextensive with the ruling apparatus,
and not widespread, and they kept a limit on it,*[11]
today when the leadership, contrary to what might be
expected in these times, is still at the disposal of
a limited group of feudal and aristocratic families
and proteges of the *court and the* two-hundred elite
families, in the style of the ancients, and our
leadership is itself a superfluous appendage to the
big political and economic powers abroad, and on the
other hand, education has expanded tremendously, and
has taken root at deeper levels of society and in a
wider range of social classes, it will surely produce
more results, *and since it only produces pencil
pushers, this inevitably means* a vastly increased
number of candidates for leadership. In such a
situation, whatever other probable characteristics
our educational system may have, more people will be
added every day to the swarm of dissatisfied individuals *who have studied and studied with the aim
of gaining staff and administrative leadership positions* until they have arrived at the threshold of
leadership but cannot find their way into leadership
positions because they lack political and financial
connections, and are neither members of one of the
two-hundred families nor major *holders of moveable
assets.*

　　　　In this situation, *as in our education,* on the
one hand the queue of those who have been trained in
the schools, universities, and in the West, with all
the faults they may have, becomes longer every day--
*meaning that the possibility of creating an extensive
intellectual environment becomes greater*--while on
the other hand the /power of the/leadership *apparatus*
becomes more closed, exclusive, and monopolistic
every day *while the Security Organization's sifting
gets harsher and more intolerant.* What can we do
about this conflict? We can see here that we live in
a time of escalating social conflict. Under such
conditions, training submissive and conformist people
and squelching violent and mutinous *human forces* is
the most dangerous and suffocating step that can be
taken to arrest change. *And the Ministry of Education is taking this step with the help of the
Security Organization and the army, with today's
Teacher's Corps and the Health Corps of the future!*

　　　　The task of education and policy in this country
at this time ought to be to help identify differences
and conflicts--conflicts between generations, between
classes, and among different schools of thought, *in*

Solution

*order at least to know what problems lie ahead. Once
the problems are clear the solutions will of course
also be found.* It is the special responsibility of
the Ministry of Education to help tear down all the
walls of obstruction within which the country's
centers of command and leadership have enclosed the
country and monopolized it. *I'm talking about making
the country's leadership 'democratic', or making a
monopoly of it for this or that person or family. I
cannot be any more explicit than this. It is the
responsibility of the Ministry of Education to* break
down every wall that's been erected in the path of
progress and evolution, and to give aid to that side
of the *intellectual, real, and human* equation that
belongs to the future, not to the side that's fading
away and has no place in our times. Our educational
and political leadership must use these active and
provocative young people as levers to dislodge these
old institutions, with all their heaviness, in the
twinkling of an eye and put them to use as materials
for building a different world. In these times of
change we need radical, principled people with personality and skills, not Weststruck people of the
type I've described. We don't need people who are
repositories of facts, jacks-of-all-trades and
masters of none, *or just nice fellows and good
people,* or who are submissive and compliant. We
don't need placid conformists or people who live
docilely in a blissful world of their own. *It is
these people who have written our history as it has
been so far. We've had enough of them.*

　The West is fortunate in that, having surpassed
the need for wizards, Aristotles, Farabis,[11] and
walking encyclopedias of human knowledge, thanks to
the work of its encyclopedists, *it no longer has a
need for this type of insect I've been describing.
It was at that point that /scientific/ division of
labor began and specialists appeared. But the expertise that the Westerner produces* is machinestruck,
and it has no personality. We must begin here.
/Although our encyclopedists have yet to be born, we
need people who are specialists and have personality
as well./ *We must begin here to train specialists
with personality.* Can our educational system train
such people? *And if it can't, why not? What is the
problem? This is what must be sought out and
eliminated.* /It's true that we train specialists in
America (and perhaps Germany), but these people are
barbarians, blown in by the wind, who will be blown
away by it as well. In Europe too (I mean in France

Solution

and England) they train this same type of specialist,
but they train boasting, self-important know-it-
alls./

If they have substituted specialization for personality in the West because of the exigencies of
capitalism and technology, *that is, because of
machinestruckness*, we have merely substituted fickle
affectation for specialization and personality because of the exigencies of Gharbzadegi. I repeat
that our schools, our educational system, and our
universities, either intentionally or out of ignorance of the times, are training these same kinds
of people and sending them into leadership positions.
They're Weststruck people with their feet in the air,
with no faith in any sense of the word, no party, no
human hopes, no tradition, and no mythology. They're
perverted, committed to a kind of poor man's
epicureanism. They cling to physical pleasures, totally occupied with sensuality and superficiality.
They all think only of today, never of tomorrow--and
all this with encouragement from the radio, the
press, books, closed laboratories, the Gharbzadegi of
the leadership, the distorted thinking of West-
returnees, and the affected knowledge of scholars of
ancient literature and tomb excavators!

Our government, which with all its power cannot
even give the illusion of tranquility in this situation, tries a new trick every day to keep the people
inattentive and sleeping. There are no more than
three kinds of these tricks no matter what they are,
which is to say that all of them fall within the
three categories of mania listed below.

First is the mania for exuding greatness, *since
every little man will see his own greatness in the
grand things they falsely attribute to him, you see.
In the grandeur* at demonstrations, at extravagant
celebrations, at flimsy arches of triumph /built in
two days./ with the crown jewels at the National
Bank, with styles of clothing, with the saddles and
harnesses of horsemen, with the tassels and tufts of
military commanders, on huge buildings *and huger dams
with endless promotion and discussion about lavishing
our national capital on their construction,* and with
anything in general that catches the eye. *Fill the
little man's eyes so he'll think he's great!*

Second is the mania for honoring the ancient
past, *although this is also an extension of the mania*

*for exuding greatness, but since it is associated
mostly with the ears I set it apart by itself. It is
a kind of mania that you mostly hear.* This is a mania
for showing off in front of strangers, for competing
in boasting vaingloriously and stupidly of Cyrus and
Darius, basking proudly in Rostam's[13] reflected
glory, *and whatever fills all the country's radio
programming and the press. This mania is something
to fill the ears. Have you ever seen a tired young
worker going home down a deserted street in the dark
of the night? You've undoubtedly heard most of them
singing? And do you know why? Because they fear
solitude. He fills his own ears with his own voice,
and thereby drives away the fear. I don't know if
you've noticed or not, but the radio has the same
function. The radio is on everywhere just to be
making a noise, to fill the ears.* /I illustrated
this last mania in my criticism of the fifth grade
elementary history book.[14] This mania, also, in all
its aspects, fills our minds!/[15]

Third is the paranoia of being pursued constantly. Every day you create a new and imaginary enemy
*for the innocent people and fill the press and radio
broadcasts with it to frighten the people, to make
them withdraw into themselves more than before, and
to persuade them to be thankful for what they have.
This continual pursuit takes different forms.* One
day it was the discovery of the Tudeh[16] party network. Another day it was the antiopium campaign,
then the antiheroin campaign, then the Bahrain situation, or a dispute with Iraq[17] *over the Shatt al-Arab
[Waterway], then there are stories of kidnappers, and
then this very terror that the shah's Security Organization instills in our hearts,* /and all of what
fills the ears in general/!

NOTES

[1]Hadaf-e Farhang-e Iran [The goal of Iranian Education], published by Markaz-e Motale'eh va Pakhsh-e Asnad-e Farhangi, *the Ministry of Education* (Tehran: Bahman, 1320 [January 21-February 19, 1962]), *the same collection that was to have been included in this booklet but could not be.* (A)

[2]Ibid. (A)

[3]*Remember that the first version of* Gharbzadegi *was written in the winter of 1340* [1961]. (A)

[4]*Voyage au bout de la nuit,* by L. F. Celine. (Paris: Gallimard, [1932]). (A) [Translators' note: Celine was the pseudonym used by Louis Ferdinand Destouches, 1894-1961.]

[5]Bandar Abbas and Qeshm Island, like the other places listed here, are scorching hot, remote locations where laborers are needed to extract natural resources, in this case oil. (tr)

[6]*An interesting point is that this exporting of gangsters is reciprocal, from the West to the East and vice versa. We've seen the European version of this so now we'll look at an example of our own, though much less frequent by comparison--the same as the ratio between our exports and our imports. The gangsters from here, too, as soon as things get hot and they're drummed out of town, following in the footsteps of those same European gangsters living here, but in more acceptable guises (orientalist, expert, dealer in artifacts, journalist, and other kinds of neocolonialist agents) pack up their bags and go to the best spots in Europe and the United States and set up camp until things blow over here and they can come back. I know this bankrupt banker from Tehran who fled to London after his bank failed and now runs a* chelow kebab *shop there. You know that bankrupt politician yourselves who was Iran's representative in UNESCO for two years, and that other one who was a roving student ambassador(!), and so on. Note also that if the export of European gangsters to the East is the sequel to exporting*

machines or a way of clearing the air in Europe of
adventurers and malcontents and of bringing about
security for the people in that sphere, here it's a
sort of perquisite and a pat on the back that the
ruling clique gives to its proteges--and what difference is there between the two? I think if it were
possible to strike out all the nonsense in this booklet, this point alone, which occurs as a comment in
the margins, is enough to verify this booklet's
claims. (A)

⁷And this rival will be everyone. Western
free(!) trade makes no distinction between friend and
enemy. In addition to the story of the wrecked tanks
the Belgians bought from the Al Alamayn battlefield
and resold to the Israelis and Egyptians after
repairing them so they could be used in another war,
note this item, which I will translate for you from
Time magazine from the United States: "The Hong Kong
Hilton was nearing its opening date when authorities
discovered that the $100,000 worth of Chinese furni-
ture and decorations in the hotel had been imported
from Red China in violation of U.S. law that American
citizens cannot deal with the Red Chinese...." From
Time magazine, July 19, 1963, p. 60. (A)

•These tribal struggles took place in 1911.
See Cottam, op. cit., chapter 4. (tr)

•The word for the traditional gymnasium is
zurkhaneh [literally, 'house of strength']. Michael
M.J. Fischer says of it, "Exercises in the zurkhana
are done to the beat of a drum and chanting of the
Shahnameh or other poetry. The exercises are
prefaced and concluded with prayers and punctuated
with salawat (praises to the family of Muhammad) and
la'nat (curses upon the enemies of Islam). In the
past ill people were brought to the zurkhana for particularly efficacious prayers and collections were
taken up there for the unfortunate of the community."
From Michael M.J. Fischer, Iran: From Religious Dispute to Revolution (Cambridge, Mass.: Harvard,
1980), p. 141. (tr)

¹⁰Marathon was originally the name of a Greek
village, in which the Greeks conquered the Persians
in 490 B.C. The first person to carry the news of
this victory from that village to Athens was hailed
as a hero. It is both in his memory and in memory of
that event that the marathon has been made the most
important Olympic event. *And then which of us knows*

who Ariobarzanes was and what heroism and valor he displayed against Alexander and his soldiers at the Takab Pass [Persian Gates] *in Fars (or I don't know where else it could have been).* (A)

¹¹*See the booklet* Hadaf-e Farhang-e Iran, *mentioned previously.* (A)

¹²al-Farabi (c. 870-950), prolific writer and one of the greatest of the early Arab philosophers, influenced by a blend of Aristotelian, neoplatonic, and Sufi thought, also known for his work on music theory, mathematics, occult science, and medicine. (tr)

¹³Rostam was a heroic mythological figure in Firdawsi's Shahnameh. (tr)

¹⁴/See "Belbeshu-ye Ketabha-ye Darsi" [The confusion in textbooks], by this writer./ (A)

¹⁵The second and third 'manias' occur in reverse order in the Muslim Students' Association edition. (tr)

¹⁶The pro-Moscow Iranian Communist party, founded in 1941, with which the author was affiliated in his youth. (tr)

¹⁷It is both sad and funny that when we were restoring the name of the Dijlih [Tigris River] to the Arvand on the radio and in the press *with the help of our scholars in the college of literature,* and *taking after Nasser, who called the Persian Gulf the Arab Gulf,* for two months the Iraqis turned back every oil tanker entering the mouth of the Shatt al-Arab bound for Abadan. This resulted in the closure of the Abadan *refinery* for two full months in 1340 [1961]. (A) [Translators' note: The Muslim Students' Association edition has "the Port of Abadan" instead of "the Abadan refinery".]

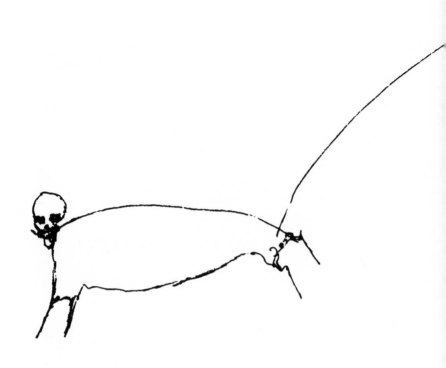

ARDESHIR. 82

11

THE HOUR OF JUDGMENT APPROACHES

The time has come to lay down the pen. Let me conclude, therefore, with a few words about some famous writers and with what seems to be a prediction but is actually the inevitable destination at the end of the road along which they are leading us and humanity.

The late French writer, Albert Camus, has written a book called <u>The Plague</u>. It may be his masterpiece. It's the story of a North African city. It is unclear why or from where the plague came to it. Maybe it was something like fate, come down from the very sky itself. At the outset, diseased and terrified mice swarm out of their holes, into the sunlit alleyways, sidewalks, and streets. In a day's time every garbage can is full of their little corpses, each one with red stains around the mouth. Then the people come down with it everywhere and die and die and die until a day comes when the sounds of hearse bells never cease, and corpses have to be taken from the living at gunpoint to be covered with lime and carried to the graveyard.

The city is quarantined, of course, and within this plague-ridden ghetto every resident of the city is looking for something. One is trying to find a cure for the plague. Another looks for a place of

refuge. Another seeks narcotics, and another tries
to take advantage of the situation.

In such a city, apart from the triumph of death
and the hopeless human struggle to escape it--and a
sadness that hovers in the air like clouds of dust--
what is most striking is that the presence of the
plague--this demon of death--only serves to quicken
each individual's pace as he or she continues to follow the same path as always. Right or wrong, moral
or immoral, the presence of the plague not only
prevents no one from taking the same path as before--
it even casts people onto that very road at a run.
Exactly like ourselves, stricken by the plague of
Gharbzadegi, who have only quickened our corrupt
footsteps.

When The Plague appeared, some of its critics
(the ones on the right) said that Camus's
plaguestruck city was a metaphor for Russian society.
Others (on the left) said that the book planted the
seeds of the Algerian revolution--and others said
many other things I neither recall nor consider per-
tinent here. When I translated the book, however, I
didn't take on the job because of these criticisms,
but in order to discover the writer's basic intentions. A third of the translation was finished when
I understood, which is to say that I saw what the
author was saying, and when the matter became clear I
abandoned the translation. I saw that the plague, in
Camus's view, was "machinism." This killer of
beauty, poetry, humanity, the future, and the sky!

I had put this experience well behind me by the
time the Frenchman Eugene Ionesco's play, Rhinoceros,
came out. Again there is a city and its people. They
all carry on with their daily lives unsuspectingly,
but suddenly an epidemic spreads over the city. Note
that like The Plague (and like Gharbzadegi/cholera)
again the theme is a contagious disease. And what is
this disease? Becoming a rhinoceros! First fever
strikes, then the voice degenerates and gets thick
and hoarse, then a horn grows out the forehead, then
the faculty of speech turns into the ability to roar
like an animal, then the skin thickens, and so on...
Everyone comes down with it: the housewife, the
grocer, the bank president, so-and-so's lover, and on
and on. They all take to the streets and run
roughshod over the city, civilization, and beauty.
This time, of course, there was no need to translate
the book to understand what this writer was saying.[1]

But I've always had it in my mind to translate this play into Persian one day and to show point by point in the commentary how the good people living with us in our city are turning into rhinoceroses too, day by day. The ultimate solution to this is to stand up to the machine.

Well and good. This was also well behind me when just recently (*in the year 1340)[1961]* I saw the film The Seventh Seal in Tehran, by the Swedish film director Ingmar Bergman, a filmmaker from the northern extremities of the Western world, a man from the regions of the polar nights. The setting of the film is another plaguestruck land in the Middle Ages. A tired, broken, and dejected knight has returned to his homeland from the Crusades. Now get this. He has returned from the Crusades where he's never discovered the truth, because he's seen the same things in the Holy Lands that his Western descendants see today in the colonized world of Africa and the East.

This cavalier, unlike the Europeans of today, had not sought *petroleum*, spices, and silk on his journey to the East. He went there to find truth, and the absolute truth at that! He had wanted to *see* and touch God in the Holy Lands *of Palestine*. Exactly like the apostles of Christ who, having imagined they had seen God, trumpeted the Christian gospel to the four corners of the world.

This Swedish cavalier, who has come from the land of the long polar nights to the astonishing bright land of the Eastern sun, is also searching for God. Instead of God, however, he found Satan in his path at every step, sometimes as a chess opponent, sometimes as a cleric, and always with the face of the angel of death, who had scattered the seeds of the plague in that land and was now reaping the souls of men.

During those days when our cavalier had wearily returned from his search for the truth, the church was invoking distressing scriptures promising the Day of Resurrection and the Hour of Judgment, soon to come. These things indicate that when the age of faith ends it will usher in a time of punishment. When the age of belief ends there will be an era of experimentation. Experimentation will lead in turn to the atomic bomb. These are Bergman's clues, *or my interpretation of them.*

Now I, the least of the least, not as an Easterner, but as a Muslim in the original tradition, who believed in the divine revelation and assumed that before dying I would stand watching the resurrected people of the world on the Plain of Judgment, can see that Albert Camus, *Eugene Ionesco*, Ingmar Bergman, and many other artists, all from the Western world, are bringing us word of this very Resurrection. They've all given up on the outcome of human activity. Sartre's Erostrate closed his eyes and fired into the crowd on the street. Nabokov's hero drove his car right at the people, and Morseau of The <u>Stranger</u> killed a man just because of the intensity of the sun's heat. These fictitious endings all reflect the true fate of humanity. *If humanity wishes to avoid being crushed by machines, it must surely don rhinoceros skins. I see that these story endings all foretell that final hour at the end of the road for humanity when the hydrogen bomb will be dropped by the machine demon (if we don't capture it first and put its spirit back in the bottle)...*

With that, I will purify my pen with this verse:

"The Hour of Judgment is nigh and the moon is cleft asunder."[2]

NOTES

[1] *Although I finally did end up doing this.* (A)

[2] The Holy Qur'an, Surah 54. v. 1 (Yusuf Ali translation). (tr)

ABOUT THE TRANSLATORS

Ahmad Alizadeh and John Green became friends as classmates at Portland State University in 1978. Their mutual interest in exploring the mysterious cultural gap between Iran and the United States has been the inspiration for several joint translation projects, both from Farsi to English and English to Farsi. They are currently working on an English rendition of Al-e Ahmad's *Khasi dar Mayqat* (Lost in the Crowd). Mr. Alizadeh has a bachelor's degree in Persian literature from Jondishapur University of Ahvaz, Iran. He is now pursuing a master's degree in sociology at Portland State University. Mr. Green did undergraduate work at Portland State University and is currently working on a Ph.D. in Persian linguistics at the University of Michigan.